CROSSBLENDS
45156 Main St. • P.O. Box 1161
Mendocino, California 95460
(707) 937-4201

THE
QUILTIE LADIES'
SCRAPBOOK

By
Variable Star Quilters

VARIABLE STAR QUILTERS

Sallie Astheimer

Sandy Barford

Ann Bean

Ann Chess

Jody Clemens

Nancy Coyle

Jan Deitcher

June Gargas

Barb Garrett

Norma Grasse

Melissa Horn

Bev Musselman

Nancy Roan

Mary Shelly

Eleanor Shubert

Sue Swartley

All due care was exercised in compiling this book but we cannot be responsible for your interpretation of any portion.

Illustrated by: *Sally Astheimer and Melissa Horn*
Photographer: *Brian McNeill*
First Printing (3,000) June 1987
Second Printing (3,500) January 1988
Third Printing (5,000) December 1988
Fourth Printing (3,000) July 1991
Fifth Printing (3,000) October 1993
Printed by Indian Valley Printing, Ltd., Souderton, PA

Profits from this publication go to charity.

For additional copies, send $12.95 per book plus $3.00
for postage, handling, (6% Sales Tax, PA only)
VARIABLE STAR QUILTERS, 16 Harbor Place, Souderton, PA 18964

INTRODUCTION

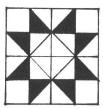

To spend time with the Variable Stars quilt group is to share in a friendly, supportive, highly creative and exciting environment.

As a friend to three and a participant in a quilting trip with the entire group, I am repeatedly in awe of their accomplishments both as individuals and as a group.

The Variable Stars grew from a core of women who took an advanced quilting course at Souder's Store, Souderton. Over lunch, at the conclusion of the sessions, someone suggested they continue to meet on their own. That was 1977.

Their monthly day-long meetings in members' homes combine show-and-tell, problem-solving and the sharing of new ideas. Their better-than-average quilting ability is nurtured by the responsiveness to and satisfaction in each other's accomplishments.

All sixteen members are linked by a Friendship Quilt Project which exemplifies the spirit of the group. Each has pieced squares for the others in order to learn new patterns and to acquire quilts of their own. The project has so far produced two quilt tops for each in the design of her choice, with round three already in progress.

It is their pride of accomplishment which has enabled them also to have six quilt shows to their credit, with a seventh coming October, 1987. The latter will include a spotlight on scrap quilts; others have focused on star patterns and a Christmas theme. Proceeds are given to local charities.

Recognition of the fine work of the group earned them the privilege of designing and piecing the raffle quilt for the 1987 National Quilting Association meeting in Easton, Pennsylvania. Wanting to reflect the local heritage of their area, they blended local patterns and traditional elements in their "Perkiomen Heritage" quilt.

That these women have now decided to "piece" a cookbook seems natural. From this project others may gain insight into the magic that piecing and quilting together has always worked on women: we all know that the completed quilt has often been secondary to the lives and friendships pieced right along with the calico and thread.

Kaaren Steiner
Quilting Friend

VARIABLE STAR QUILTERS

Many friendships have developed among the Variable Star Quilters since the group's beginning. Now with the publication of this book we hope to widen our circle of quilting friends. The *Quiltie Ladies' Scrapbook* is a collection of recipes, quilt designs and numerous other scraps of information that might be of interest to other "quiltie ladies". This unusual or unique name has been given us by the young son of one of our members. Enjoy the *Quiltie Ladies' Scrapbook*.

Our lives are albums written through
With good or ill, with false or true;
And as the blessed angels turn
The pages of our years,
God grant they read the good with smiles,
And blot the ill with tears!

Whittier—written in a Lady's Album

WANDERING VARIABLE STAR©
Pattern on page 152

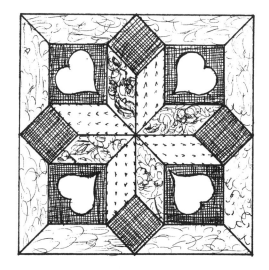

FRIENDSHIP STAR©
Pattern on page 151

JANUARY

SUNDAY	MONDAY	TUESDAY	WEDNESDAY	THURSDAY	FRIDAY	SATURDAY
			Philadelphia Pavement			
	Take that Christmas tree down and pack up those holiday trappings, put up the quilting frame, and get on with some serious quilting.			Listen very carefully to the weather report—don't get caught in a big snowstorm without sufficient fabric. When heavy snow is forecast, shop for fabric first, then get the bread and milk, if you have time.	**Snowball**	
			Winter Landscape			
You will never "find" time for anything. If you want time, you must make it. Charles Buxton						

5

O the snow, the beautiful snow,
Filling the sky and the earth below.
Over the house-tops, over the street,
Over the heads of the people you meet,
      Dancing,
      Flirting,
      Skimming along,
Beautiful snow, it can do nothing wrong.

John Whitaker Watson

QUILTERS LUNCHEON

*LASAGNE ROLL-UPS ***
*QUILTIE LADIES SALAD BOWL ***
*DELI ROLL BREAD ***
*LEMON CAKE PUDDING ***

We've enjoyed the Lasagne Rolls at a quilt meeting luncheon. Obviously the bread could be omitted for the sake of time or calories, but it's January and homemade bread warms the house as well as the soul. Bake the Lemon Pudding in a single large casserole if you prefer, but don't forget to place it in a pan of water while baking to guarantee a delicate texture.

LASAGNE ROLL-UPS

12 lasagne noodles (cooked)
¾ cup chopped onion
2 tablespoons butter
1¼ cups cottage cheese
1½ cups Cheddar cheese (shredded)
1 package chopped broccoli (10 ounces) (cooked and drained)
¼ teaspoon seasoned salt
⅛ teaspoon garlic powder
⅛ teaspoon pepper
1 tablespoon flour
½ cup grated Parmesan cheese
2 cans pizza sauce (8 ounces each)

Saute onions in butter. Beat cottage cheese for 5 minutes at high speed in mixer. Add ¼ cup Cheddar cheese, broccoli, seasoned salt and onion. Combine Parmesan cheese with flour, set aside. Spread ¼ cup cheese filling on each noodle, sprinkle with Parmesan cheese mixture. Roll up in jelly roll fashion.

Put small amount of pizza sauce in bottom of 9 x 13-inch pan, arrange roll-ups in pan, cover with remaining sauce. Bake at 350° for 30 minutes. Remove from oven and sprinkle with remaining Cheddar cheese. Reheat for 3 minutes. Serves 6

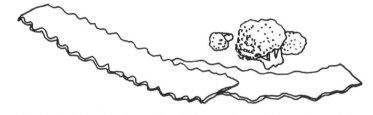

QUILTIE LADIES' SALAD BOWL

Salad:

1 cup frozen green peas
1 cucumber (thinly sliced)
½ cup chopped green onions
¼ cup chopped celery
assorted lettuces

Dressing:

¼ cup salad oil
¼ cup vinegar
1 tablespoon sugar
1 small garlic clove (chopped)
½ teaspoon salt
¼ teaspoon oregano
⅛ teaspoon black pepper

Pour boiling water on peas and let stand for a few minutes. Combine lettuces and other vegetables in a large bowl. Sprinkle with drained peas. Combine dressing ingredients and pour over salad and toss just before serving.

DELI ROLL BREAD

1¼ cups warm water
2 packages dry yeast
1 tablespoon sugar
1 tablespoon melted butter
1½ teaspoons salt
3½ cups flour (approximately)
½ pound pepperoni (slivered)
½ cup cheese (shredded)

Stir yeast and sugar into warm water. Let stand until bubbly. Add the salt and about half of the flour to make a soft sticky dough. Let rise until double. Stir down and add enough remaining flour so dough can be handled. Knead on lightly floured surface until smooth and elastic, adding flour only if necessary. Cover the ball of dough and let sit 10-15 minutes. Roll into 14 x 16-inch rectangle. Spread with slivered pepperoni, cheese, and herbs of your choice. Sprinkle liberally with fresh grated black pepper. Roll as you would a jelly roll, sealing edge by pinching. Form the roll into a circle and place in a well-greased round pan. A cast iron fry pan works well. Let rise for one (1) hour. Bake at 375° for 30 minutes. Brush with melted butter.

LEMON CAKE PUDDING

¾ cup sugar
3 tablespoons all purpose flour
2 tablespoons butter or margarine (melted)
1 teaspoon grated lemon rind
⅓ cup lemon juice (fresh)
2 eggs (separated)
1¼ cups milk

Preheat oven to 325°. Mix sugar and flour in medium-size bowl, stir in melted butter, lemon rind and juice. Beat egg yolks with milk until blended, stir into lemon mixture. Beat egg whites until they form peaks, fold into egg yolk mixture. Pour into six (6) buttered 6-ounce custard cups. Set cups, not touching, in a large shallow baking pan, pour hot water into pan to a depth of one inch. Bake for 50 minutes or until desserts are golden and firm on top. Remove cups from water and cool. Serve warm or cold. Serves 6

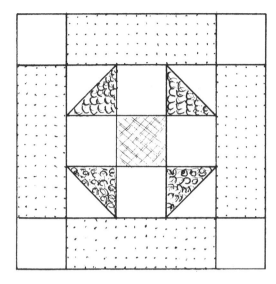

PHILADELPHIA PAVEMENT
Pattern on page 99

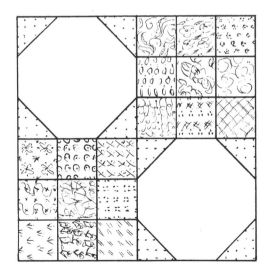

SNOWBALL
Pattern on page 100

COLD WEATHER CHOWDER SUPPER

*CLAM CORN CHOWDER ***
*BLT SALAD ***
*APPLE MUFFINS ***
FRESH FRUIT

What a perfect supper to serve by the hearth (or at the kitchen table) on a snowy night. Nothing warms the cockles of the heart like a steaming bowl of chowder, except maybe a quilt. Try both.

CLAM CORN CHOWDER

2 cans minced clams (7 ounces each)
3 slices bacon (chopped)
½ cup onions (chopped)
3½ cups raw potatoes (diced)
3 cups milk
2 tablespoons flour

1 tablespoon butter (melted)
1 teaspoon celery salt
1 teaspoon salt
dash pepper
2 cups whole kernel corn

Drain clams and combine clam liquor with enough water to measure one cup. Pan fry bacon until crisp. Add onion and saute until tender but not brown. Add potatoes and combined clam liquor and water. Cover and simmer gently until potatoes are tender (about 15 minutes).

Add corn and milk.* Blend flour and butter and stir into soup. Cook slowly until mixture thickens slightly, stirring constantly. Add seasonings and clams and simmer for five minutes. Serve hot.

*Instead of milk, part half and half may be used. To increase clam flavor, add a bottle of clam juice.

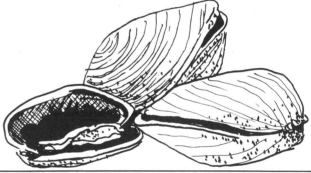

BLT SALAD

1 medium head of lettuce or lettuce and spinach mixed
1 cup croutons
1 tomato (cut up)
¼ cup small onion slices
9 slices bacon (cooked and crumbled)

Dressing:

⅓ cup salad dressing
¼ teaspoon basil
1½ teaspoon lemon juice
salt and pepper to taste

Combine dressing ingredients and pour over salad just before serving.

APPLE MUFFINS

¾ cup sugar
½ cup margarine
1 cup milk
1 egg
1½ cups flour

⅛ teaspoon salt
2 teaspoons baking powder
½ teaspoon cinnamon
1 teaspoon lemon juice
1 cup grated apple
cinnamon sugar

Cream sugar and margarine. Add rest of ingredients in order given being careful not to stir too much. Fill greased or lined muffin tins ⅔ full. Sprinkle with cinnamon sugar. Bake at 425° for 20-25 minutes. Makes about 20 muffins.

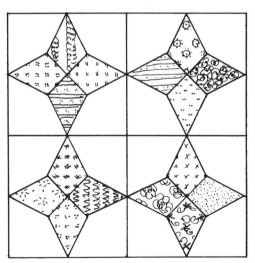

WINTER LANDSCAPE
Pattern on page 101

FEBRUARY

SUNDAY	MONDAY	TUESDAY	WEDNESDAY	THURSDAY	FRIDAY	SATURDAY
	February second is Groundhog Day. Tradition says that if the groundhog sees his shadow, there will be six more weeks of winter—good news for the quilter.					
			A stitch in time saves embarrassment.		Cupid's Arrow	
Sweetheart Honey Bee©					I eat my peas with honey, I've done it all my life. It makes the peas taste funny, But it keeps them on the knife.	
		President's Star		Set all things in their own peculiar place, And know that order is the greatest grace. Dryden		
					Keep your face to the sunshine and you cannot see the shadow. Helen Keller	

11

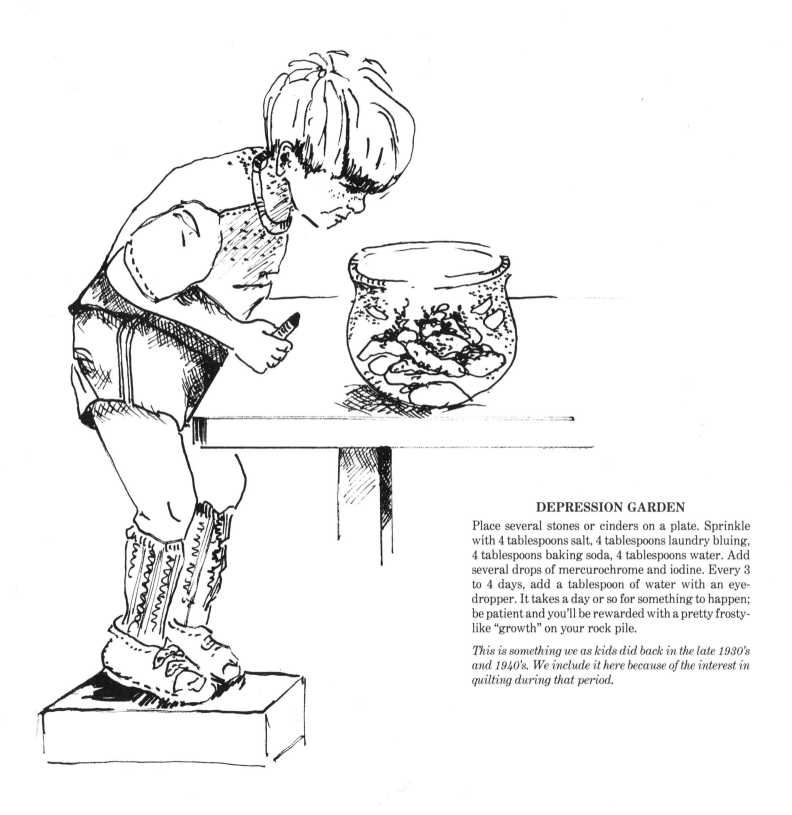

DEPRESSION GARDEN

Place several stones or cinders on a plate. Sprinkle with 4 tablespoons salt, 4 tablespoons laundry bluing, 4 tablespoons baking soda, 4 tablespoons water. Add several drops of mercurochrome and iodine. Every 3 to 4 days, add a tablespoon of water with an eyedropper. It takes a day or so for something to happen; be patient and you'll be rewarded with a pretty frosty-like "growth" on your rock pile.

This is something we as kids did back in the late 1930's and 1940's. We include it here because of the interest in quilting during that period.

PASTA SUPPER WITH A DIFFERENCE

*ZITI AND SAUSAGE ***

*DRESSING FOR GREEN SALAD ***

ROLLS

*BAKED PINEAPPLE ***

OR

*PEACH CUSTARD CAKE ***

For those who live in the non-Italian neighborhood, ziti is a type of tubular pasta. Try this sauce, a departure from the usual, on any pasta you like, or have around the house.

ZITI AND SAUSAGE

1 pound cooked ziti
1 pound sweet Italian sausage
3 tablespoons chopped onion
1 tablespoon vegetable oil
2 tablespoons butter
1½ cups heavy cream (light cream may be used)
½ teaspoon salt
¼ cup grated Parmesan cheese

Saute onion in oil and butter until golden, remove from pan. Remove casing from sausage and cook meat for 10 minutes or until browned. Stir in sauted onion and remaining ingredients and heat over low/medium heat until mixture is thick and bubbly. Serves 6

DRESSING FOR GREEN SALAD

Blend in Blender:

½ small onion
1 cup vegetable oil
½ cup ketchup

Add:

¼ cup sugar
3 tablespoons water
1 tablespoon vinegar
½ teaspoon salt

2½ tablespoons lemon juice
1 tablespoon Worcestershire sauce
1½ teaspoons celery seed
1 teaspoon paprika

Blend again until well mixed. Makes 2 cups

BAKED PINEAPPLE

1 tablespoon cornstarch
¼ cup sugar
1 extra large or 2 medium eggs
1 can crushed pineapple and juice (20 ounces)
1 tablespoon butter
cinnamon (optional)

Mix the first four ingredients in the order given and pour into a greased 2½ quart baking dish. Dot with butter. Sprinkle with cinnamon if desired. Cover and bake at 350° for 20 minutes, reduce heat to 325°, uncover dish and bake 30 minutes longer. Serves 4

PEACH CUSTARD CAKE

½ cup flour
½ cup butter
1 can sliced peaches (drained) (1 pound-13 ounces)
½ cup syrup from peaches
½ cup sugar
½ teaspoon cinnamon
1 cup evaporated milk
1 egg (slightly beaten)

Blend butter into flour and press into bottom and half way up sides of 8-inch square pan. Arrange peaches on crust. Mix sugar and cinnamon and sprinkle on peaches. Bake at 375° for 20 minutes. Beat together ½ cup peach syrup, evaporated milk and egg. Pour over hot peaches and return to oven for 30 minutes longer or until custard is firm. Center will set up more as it cools. Serve warm or cold. Serves 9

CUPID'S ARROW
Pattern on page 102

SWEETHEART HONEY BEE©
Pattern on page 103

A HEARTY WINTER MEAL

MEATLOAF AND STRING BEANS *

QUILTER'S POTATOES *

SAUERKRAUT SALAD *

CHERRY CHOCOLATE CAKE *

OR

CHERRY CAKE *

This hearty stick to the ribs dinner should please the entire family. Substitute your own favorite meat loaf recipe for ours if you desire. Either of the cakes are perfect for a tribute to George Washington. Did you know that his wife Martha's quilt (at least she is thought to have made it) is in the collection at Mt. Vernon?

MEATLOAF AND STRING BEANS

2 pounds ground beef
2 eggs (slightly beaten)
1 cup milk
1 tablespoon horseradish
2 tablespoons onion (minced)
¼ teaspoon pepper
2 teaspoons salt
1 cup bread crumbs
1 can crushed tomatoes (1 pound, 13 ounces)
3 cups string beans (fresh, frozen or leftover) (cut)

Make a meatloaf from the first eight (8) ingredients and place in the middle of a roasting pan. Bake at 350° for ½ hour. Add tomatoes and string beans and bake ½ hour longer or until string beans are done. Serves 6-8

QUILTER'S POTATOES

Wash, but do not peel, twice the quantity of potatoes your family normally eats. (These are so good you'll need them). Slice into ¼ inch slices and place in a well-buttered casserole. Sprinkle with salt and pepper as you go. Pour 3-4 tablespoons melted butter over potatoes. Cover and bake at 375° for 45 minutes. Quantity may alter this time somewhat.

SAUERKRAUT SALAD

1 pound sauerkraut (drained)
½ cup celery (chopped fine)
½ cup green pepper (chopped)
¼ cup onions (chopped fine)
¾ cup sugar
⅓ cup salad oil
⅓ cup vinegar

Mix all ingredients. Refrigerate overnight.

CHERRY CHOCOLATE CAKE

1 box chocolate cake mix
1 can cherry pie filling
2 beaten eggs

Mix thoroughly and pour into 9 x 13-inch greased and floured pan. Bake at 350° for 35 to 40 minutes.

Frosting:

5 tablespoons margarine
6 ounces chocolate chips
⅓ cup milk
1 cup sugar

Boil margarine, sugar, and milk for one minute. Add chocolate chips and stir to melt. Pour over hot cake.

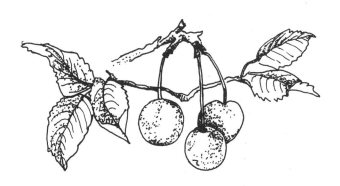

CHERRY CAKE

½ pound margarine
2 cups sugar
4 eggs
1 tablespoon vanilla
3 cups flour

1 teaspoon baking powder
dash salt
1 can cherry pie filling
1 teaspoon almond extract

Cream margarine and sugar. Add eggs, one at a time, blending well after each addition. Add vanilla. Combine flour, baking powder and salt, and add to creamed mixture. Combine pie filling and almond extract. Pour ¾ of cake batter into a greased 9 x 13-inch pan. Put cherry pie filling over batter, then spread remaining cake batter on top. Bake at 350° for 40-45 minutes or until it tests done.

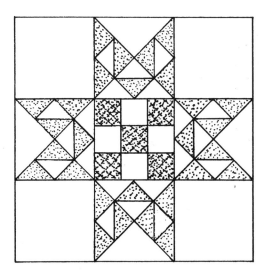

PRESIDENT'S STAR
Pattern on page 104

MARCH

SUNDAY	MONDAY	TUESDAY	WEDNESDAY	THURSDAY	FRIDAY	SATURDAY
	Blow, winds, and crack your cheeks! rage! blow! Shakespeare	**Windblown Square**				
Kites rise highest against the wind, not with it. Winston Churchill		Don't let the Ides of March get to you—start a new quilting project.		**Lucky Irish Chain©**		
	March twenty-first is the first day of spring. Fabric shopping is a sure cure for spring fever.				Nature, like a kind and smiling mother, lends herself to our dreams and cherishes our fancies. Victor Hugo	

Jack In The Pulpit

QUILT PATTERN

Nature sewed the winter through,
    Left-overs of gold and blue
From the sky . . . cerise and red
    Stitched with white and silver thread.

Patiently she stitched along
    To the north wind's lusty song. . .
Back and forth her needle flew
    While the boist'rous March winds blew.

April dawned . . . the thing was done!
    So she laid it in the sun.
Hills and gardens then were gay
    With the patchwork quilt that lay. . .

Bright, and tufted deep with green,
    Bordered with a brooklet's sheen. . .
Summer coverlet of scraps
    Garnered from autumn's leafy wraps!

Crystal Hastings
*Needlecraft and Home
Arts* Magazine,
March 1927

FOR KIDS OF ALL AGES

*PIZZA FONDUE ***
*EASY ITALIAN BREAD ***
*GREEN SALAD WITH POPPY SEED DRESSING ***
VANILLA ICE CREAM WITH MANDARIN
ORANGES SPRINKLED WITH COCONUT

Everybody, even your kids, will love this. It's easy too. Make your own Italian bread or buy it, we won't tell. Noodles are fine instead of the bread.

PIZZA FONDUE

1 onion (chopped)
½ pound ground beef
1 clove garlic (minced)
2 cups seasoned tomato sauce
1 tablespoon cornstarch
1 teaspoon oregano
10 ounces Cheddar cheese (grated)
1 cup grated Mozzarella cheese
¼ cup grated Parmesan cheese

Saute onion and garlic, add ground beef and cook until meat is done. Drain excess fat. Add remaining ingredients except cheese and cook until thickened. Stir in cheeses. Serve hot over chunks of Italian bread.

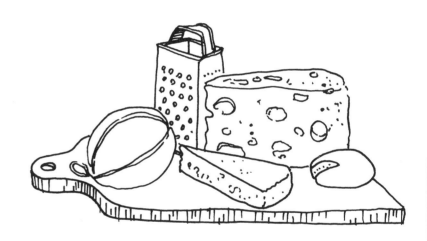

EASY ITALIAN BREAD

Make dough as for Deli Roll Bread (page 8) and shape it into long loaves or dinner size rolls. Place on cookie sheet sprinkled with corn meal, or omit corn meal and grease sheet. Bake at 400° for 15-20 minutes depending on size. Breads are done when they sound hollow when tapped.

POPPY SEED DRESSING

1¼ cups sugar
2 teaspoons dry mustard
2 teaspoons salt
⅔ cup vinegar
3 tablespoons onion juice or finely minced onion
2 cups salad oil
3 tablespoons poppy seeds

Mix first four ingredients. Add onion juice and stir it in thoroughly. Add oil slowly beating constantly until thick. Use blender or mixer for this. Add poppy seeds and beat until well blended.

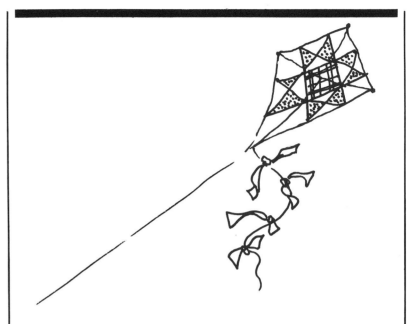

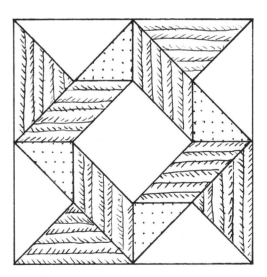

WIND BLOWN SQUARE
Pattern on page 105

LUNCHEON FOR QUILTING FRIENDS

CREAMED CHICKEN CASSEROLE *

CRANBERRY RELISH *

SPINACH SALAD *

SADIE'S CHOCOLATE CAKE *

OR

POUND CAKE *

You'll find it difficult to choose between the chocolate cake and the pound cake. Somewhat akin to choosing between two "yummy" fabrics. You could just settle for ice cream and use the extra time to quilt.

CREAMED CHICKEN CASSEROLE

3 whole chicken breasts
celery and onion
1 cup sour cream (or plain yogurt)
1 can mushroom soup
¼ pound butter
1 cup chicken broth
1-8 ounce package Pepperidge Farm Stuffing Mix.

Stew chicken in salted water with some celery and onion for 45 minutes to an hour. Cool and cube meat, retaining one cup of broth. Mix soup and sour cream (and/or yogurt). Add cubed chicken. Mix melted butter, stuffing and broth. Put a layer of the stuffing mix on bottom of greased casserole; then add chicken mixture, ending with a layer of stuffing mixture on top. Bake at 350° for 45 minutes. Leftover chicken or turkey can be used.

CRANBERRY RELISH

½ pound cranberries
¾ cup sugar
1 orange, cut in sections (do not peel)
½ cup walnuts (chopped)
1 box strawberry gelatin (4 ounce serving size)

Make gelatin according to directions, let thicken slightly (1¼-1½ hours). Chop cranberries and orange sections in blender. Combine with sugar and nuts; fold into thickened gelatin. Pour into 4-cup mold and chill.

SPINACH SALAD

1 pound bean sprouts
2 pounds spinach
2 hard boiled eggs (sliced)
8 large mushrooms (sliced)
2 medium red onions (sliced)
6 slices bacon (cooked and crumbled)

Layer the above ingredients in a large bowl. Serve with dressing.

Dressing:

⅔ cup oil
¼ cup cider vinegar
¼ cup ketchup
3 tablespoons honey
½ teaspoon salt

1 teaspoon dry mustard
1 teaspoon celery seed
1 teaspoon sesame oil
1 teaspoon celery salt

Blend all ingredients together.

SADIE'S CHOCOLATE CAKE

2 cups sugar
2 cups flour
2 teaspoons baking soda
1 teaspoon salt
¾ cup cocoa
1 teaspoon baking powder

½ cup oil
1 cup hot coffee (brewed or instant)
1 cup milk
1 teaspoon vanilla
2 eggs

Combine and mix all the ingredients. Bake in 9 x 13-inch greased and floured pan at 350° for 45 minutes. Batter will be very thin. This is a moist, not too sweet, dark chocolate cake and is so good without icing.

POUND CAKE

1 cup butter (softened)
8 ounces cream cheese (softened)
1½ cups sugar
4 eggs
1½ teaspoons vanilla
2 cups flour
1½ teaspoons baking powder

Cream butter and cream cheese. Beat in sugar until light and lemon colored. Add eggs one at a time, beating 10 seconds after each addition. Add vanilla. Combine flour and baking powder, add to creamed mixture. Pour into greased and floured 10″ tube pan. Bake at 300° for one hour. Serves 12

22

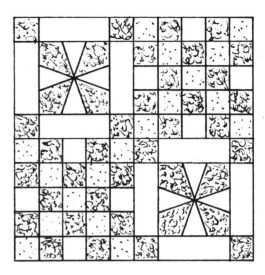

LUCKY IRISH CHAIN©
Pattern on page 106

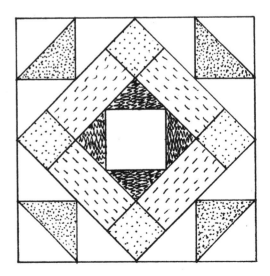

JACK IN THE PULPIT
Pattern on page 107

APRIL

SUNDAY	MONDAY	TUESDAY	WEDNESDAY	THURSDAY	FRIDAY	SATURDAY
	Arbor Day is the time to plant a tree. Find the Fir Tree pattern and make a quilt for Arbor Day but only after planting a real tree. You'll feel good— your tree quilt will grow faster than the live one.				**Spider Web**	
		Economy		Spring is plowing time. Set your Log Cabin quilt in a Straight Furrows setting.	Don't bake on Good Friday—nobody would eat it, not even the fish. So say the Pennsylvania Dutch people.	

Sunbunny Sue©	Plough deep while sluggards sleep.
	   Benjamin Franklin
	(Get up early to quilt.)
				April's anger is swift to fall
				April's wonder is worth it all.
				   Sir Henry Newbolt
				Pennsylvania Tulip©		

LIFE'S A PATCHWORK

Stitch a little bit of lovin',
Add a lot of tender care;
Sew together with some kindness.
Let the sun shine everywhere.
Choose a pattern for your life's work,
Add some fun along the way.
Life is like a valued patchwork.
Keep it precious day by day.

Anonymous

AN ELEGANT MENU FOR COMPANY

SHRIMP CREOLE *

RICE   PEAS

MY SISTER'S TOSSED SALAD *

FRENCH BREAD

CHEESECAKE *

This is a very colorful meal. Obviously each item is great on its own, so feel free to juggle anyway you like. The cheesecake is a simple version but lacks nothing in quality.

SHRIMP CREOLE

2 pounds shelled and deveined shrimp
4 tablespoons butter
1 large onion (chopped)
1 green pepper (chopped)
1 cup chopped celery
1 large can crushed tomatoes
2 teaspoons salt
2 bay leaves
1 teaspoon thyme
½ teaspoon Tabasco sauce

Saute onions and pepper in butter until golden. Add celery and tomatoes. Bring to boil. Reduce heat and add seasonings. Simmer for 15 minutes. Add raw shrimp and simmer 5 minutes or until shrimp are fully cooked. Serve over cooked rice. Serves 6-8

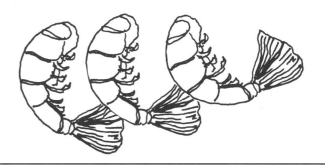

MY SISTER'S TOSSED SALAD

8 cups torn romaine lettuce
¼ cup vegetable oil
¾ cup sour cream
½ teaspoon salt
⅛ teaspoon onion salt
1 clove garlic (minced)

tabasco to taste
1 teaspoon white vinegar
1 teaspoon fresh lemon juice
½ cup grated Parmesan cheese
2 cups croutons

Combine oil and sour cream in small bowl. Add salt, garlic, onion salt and Tabasco. Combine vinegar and lemon juice, gradually stir into oil/sour cream mixture. Stir in ¼ cup Parmesan cheese, let stand one hour. To serve: place greens in bowl with remaining Parmesan cheese. Toss lightly with salad dressing until well coated. Add croutons. Serves 6

CHEESECAKE

2 packages Philadelphia cream cheese
3 eggs
¾ cup sugar
1 teaspoon vanilla

Topping:
¾ cup sour cream
¼ cup sugar
1 teaspoon vanilla

Beat together cream cheese, eggs, ¾ cup sugar and 1 teaspoon vanilla. Pour into greased 9-inch glass pie plate. Bake at 350° for 20 minutes. Let sit for 10 minutes. Make topping by combining topping ingredients. Spread on cheesecake and return to oven for 15 minutes. Chill before serving.

No woman does her housework with real joy unless she is in love—and a woman may go being quietly in love for fifty years almost without knowing it.

D. H. Lawrence

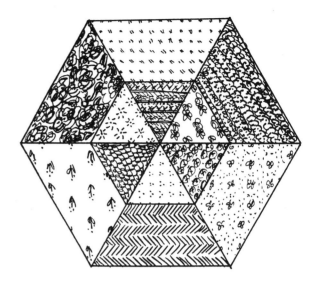

SPIDER WEB
Pattern on page 109

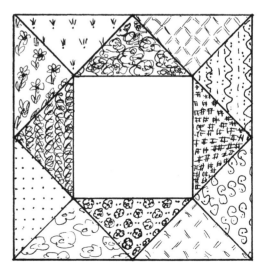

ECONOMY
Pattern on page 110

AFTER EASTER LUNCH

HOT DEVILED EGGS *

MATTHEW'S GREEN BEANS *

MUSHROOM SALAD *

HUBBY'S BREAD *

FRESH FRUIT OR SHERBET

Here's a solution to all of those hard-cooked eggs left by the Easter Bunny. The string beans are the very favorite food of a twelve year old Matthew—excluding pizza, of course.

It is not raining rain to me,
It's raining daffodils;
In every dimpled drop I see
Wild flowers on distant hills.

April Rain
Robert Loveman

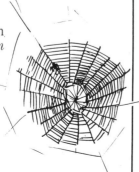

HOT DEVILED EGGS

6-8 hard boiled eggs
3 tablespoons sour cream
2½ teaspoons prepared mustard
¼ teaspoon salt

Sauce:

2 tablespoons butter
⅓ cup chopped onion
1 cup sour cream
1 can mushroom soup

½ cup chopped mushrooms
½ cup shredded cheese
paprika

Slice eggs lengthwise, remove yolks, and devil using sour cream, mustard, and salt. Fill egg whites. Melt butter in large skillet, saute onion and mushrooms until tender. Remove from heat, stir in soup and sour cream. Put eggs in 1½ quart shallow baking dish. Pour sauce over eggs, sprinkle with cheese and paprika. Bake in 350° oven for 25 minutes. Can be made ahead. Serves 6-8

MATTHEW'S GREEN BEANS

1 pound green beans (cleaned and cut into 1-inch pieces)
1 tablespoon oil
1 medium onion (chopped)
1 small clove garlic (finely minced)
crushed tomatoes (15-ounce can)
pinch of oregano and pinch of basil

Cook beans in salted water until about half done. Drain. Saute onion and garlic in oil until onion is golden. Combine with beans, tomatoes, and herbs. Simmer until beans are tender. Add salt and pepper to taste. Grated Parmesan cheese is nice sprinkled on top when serving.

MUSHROOM SALAD

3 cans mushrooms (8 ounces each)
1½ cups salad olives
¼ teaspoon pepper
2 tablespoons parsley (chopped)
1 cup oil
1 teaspoon celery salt

1 can artichoke hearts
1½ cups chopped celery
2 tablespoons oregano
¾ cup white vinegar
3 cloves crushed garlic

Mix all ingredients together and refrigerate. This salad is better if made one day before serving.

HUBBY'S BREAD

3 cups All-Bran cereal
¼ cup Crisco
3 cups boiling water
1 cup lukewarm water
1 cup sugar
2 packages dry yeast
8 cups flour
2 teaspoons salt

Combine cereal, Crisco, and boiling water and let cool until lukewarm. Combine lukewarm water, sugar and yeast and let sit until yeast is dissolved. Stir yeast mixture into cereal mixture, add flour and salt until all is well combined. Let rise. Stir down and pour into three greased loaf pans. Let rise. Bake at 425° for 15 minutes, reduce temperature to 350° and bake 45 minutes longer.

SUNBUNNY SUE©
Pattern on page 111

PENNSYLVANIA TULIP©
Pattern on page 112

MAY

SUNDAY	MONDAY	TUESDAY	WEDNESDAY	THURSDAY	FRIDAY	SATURDAY
We each have a choice... We can stay under a cloud or get busy and find our rainbow. Joan Walsh Anglund		**Milady's Basket**				
					Bird's Nest	A bird in hand is bad table manners.
Mother's Delight			Dear little one, I wish you two things: To give you roots, To give you wings. Author Unknown			
		Don't sew on Ascension Day.				
					Patch Puss	

29

A FRIEND BY YOUR SIDE

Close by my machine on the table sat,
Neat stacks of patches, and my pussy cat.
I'd carefully planned for a good sewing day,
But pussy's concept of patchwork is play.

He wanted my company, my attention and me.
And messin' my patches, my attention—got he!
Red triangles, blue squares, can be tossed up so neatly,
By deft little paws with a look that says sweetly,

"I'm helping you work by arranging the pieces.
So sorry for where I've sat and made creases."
He stayed and watched as my machine buzzed away.
Then an occasional yawn, his intent did betray.

Patches became squares, the pile was growing,
As pussy succumbed to the sandman, I continued my
      sewing.
Sewing was easier since behind those little paws he
      did hide,
But in spite of the hassle—it's always so nice to have a
      friend by your side.

LUNCH WITH MOTHER

HOT CHICKEN SALAD CASSEROLE *
CARROT SALAD *
EASY NO-KNEAD ROLLS *
APPLESAUCE CAKE ROLL *

Delight your mother, or anybody's mother, with this delicious Chicken Salad Casserole. Plan to mix the rolls a day or two ahead. Won't Mother be surprised by fresh baked rolls?

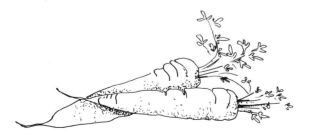

HOT CHICKEN SALAD CASSEROLE

8 chicken breasts
1 bottle French dressing (Wishbone's French with garlic) (8 ounces)
1 cup chopped celery
1 cup mayonnaise
1-1 pound jar soft cheese spread (Cheese Whiz)
1 can French-fried onions
optional–1 cup chopped almonds or pecans

The day before serving, boil chicken breasts, cool, remove meat from bones and cut into bite-sized pieces. Toss in French dressing and marinate overnight. Next day, add celery and mayonnaise to taste (be generous with the mayonnaise) to make chicken salad. Add nuts if desired. Place salad in a baking dish and spread with cheese spread. Bake in 350° oven for ½ hour. Sprinkle can of French-fried onions on top and bake 5 minutes longer.

CARROT SALAD

2 pounds carrots (sliced)
1 green pepper (chopped)
1 onion (chopped)
1 cup tomato soup
½ cup oil
½ cup vinegar
1 teaspoon Worcestershire sauce
salt and pepper to taste
1 teaspoon prepared mustard

Alternate layers of carrots, pepper and onion. Make a sauce with soup, oil, sugar, vinegar, Worcestershire, salt, pepper and mustard. Heat until well blended. Pour hot mixture over vegetables and refrigerate several days. Serves 8

EASY NO-KNEAD ROLLS

1 cup hot water
½ cup Crisco
¼ cup sugar
1 teaspoon salt

1 package dry yeast
½ cup lukewarm water
1 egg
4 cups flour
butter
cinnamon sugar

Heat water, Crisco, sugar and salt until Crisco is melted. Cool to lukewarm. Dissolve yeast in lukewarm water. Add to Crisco mixture. Stir in egg and flour. Mix well and refrigerate. About 2 hours before baking, remove from refrigerator to warm to room temperature. Roll dough into a 12 x 15-inch rectangle, spread with butter and sprinkle with cinnamon sugar. Roll up and slice into ¾-inch slices and place each into greased muffin cups. Let rise until light. Bake at 400° for 15 minutes. Make the dough a day or two before using. Makes 20 rolls

APPLESAUCE CAKE ROLL

1 cup flour
½ teaspoon baking powder
½ teaspoon baking soda
¼ teaspoon salt
¼ teaspoon cloves
½ teaspoon cinnamon
3 eggs
¾ cup sugar
½ cup applesauce
¼ cup raisins

Sift dry ingredients together. Beat eggs and sugar until thick and fluffy. Gently fold the dry ingredients into egg mixture. Add applesauce and raisins. Line jelly roll pan with greased wax paper. Pour in batter. Bake in 375° oven for 15-20 minutes. Turn cake onto a sugar sprinkled towel, remove wax paper and roll up in towel and let cool.

Filling:

1-8 ounce package cream cheese
2 teaspoons milk
¼ cup sugar

Mix together and spread on cool cake. Roll as for jelly roll. Wrap in wax paper tightly and refrigerate.

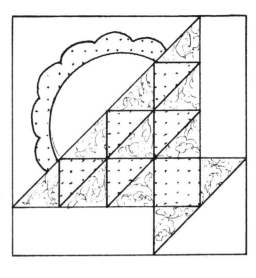

MILADY'S BASKET
Pattern on page 113

BIRD'S NEST
Pattern on page 114

BARBEQUE INDOORS OR OUT

---

*BARBEQUED SPARE RIBS ***
BUTTERED NOODLES
*AUNT CONNIE'S PICKLED CABBAGE ***
*PRUNE CAKE ***

Make the cake the night before, let the ribs cook in the crock pot all day while you fabric shop or quilt. Maybe your husband will take over and grill them at dinner time. Tell him fabric shopping is tiring.

BARBEQUED SPARE RIBS

1 onion (chopped)	*1 cup water*
1 clove garlic (chopped)	*1½ cups chopped celery*
2 tablespoons vinegar	*3 teaspoons salt*
1 tablespoon orange juice	*1 teaspoon mustard*
6 tablespoons brown sugar	*1 teaspoon cinnamon*
2 cups ketchup	*4 teaspoons Worcestershire sauce*
5 pounds country style ribs	*crushed pineapple (optional)*

Mix all ingredients together. Cook ribs in this mixture until ribs are done. This works well in a slow-cooker on low setting all day. Remove ribs from sauce and broil to brown if desired. Leftover sauce is good for use in hamburger barbeque.

AUNT CONNIE'S PICKLED CABBAGE

1 head cabbage (shredded)
2 cups sugar
1 cup white vinegar
¼ cup water
celery salt
pepper

Boil sugar, vinegar and water for 3 minutes. Cool. Pour cooled syrup over shredded cabbage. Add celery salt and pepper to taste.

PRUNE CAKE

1½ cups sugar
¼ cup butter
¼ cup Crisco
3 eggs (beaten)
3 cups flour
2 teaspoons baking soda
1 teaspoon cinnamon
1 teaspoon nutmeg
1 teaspoon cloves
1 cup prune juice
1 cup cut-up pitted prunes

Cream sugar, butter and Crisco. Stir in eggs. Sift flour, soda, and spices together. Add dry ingredients to creamed mixture alternately with prune juice. Stir in prunes. Pour batter into two 9-inch greased and floured pans. Bake at 350° for 30 minutes. Cool and frost if desired.

A fair little girl sat under a tree,
Sewing as long as her eyes could see;
Then smoothed her work, and folded it right,
And said, "Dear work, good-night, good-night."

Good Night and Good Morning
Richard Monckton Milnes

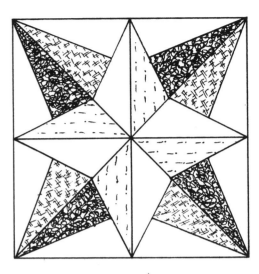

MOTHER'S DELIGHT
Pattern on page 116

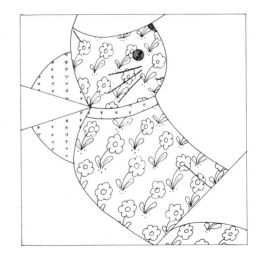

PATCH-PUSS
Pattern on page 117

JUNE

SUNDAY	MONDAY	TUESDAY	WEDNESDAY	THURSDAY	FRIDAY	SATURDAY
		"I think old-time patchwork too pretty and useful an accomplishment to have gone out of fashion . . ." Aunt Sarah *Mary at the Farm*, Edith M. Thomas, Quakertown, 1915				 **Bride's Choice**
 Crab©				June 14—Flag Day—Fly "Old Glory." Did you ever consider making a flag? Betsy Ross did and she was only a seamstress.		
Father's Day—Make a Bow Tie quilt for Dad.		 **Strawberry Basket©**		June 21—1st Day of Summer.		
		A little nonsense now and then Is relished by the wisest men. Anonymous				 **Old Maid's Puzzle**

The best verse hasn't been rhymed yet,
The best house hasn't been planned,
The highest peak hasn't been climbed yet,
The mightiest rivers aren't spanned;
Don't worry and fret, faint-hearted,
The chances have just begun
For the best jobs haven't been started,
The best work hasn't been done.

No Chance
Berton Braley

ENTERTAIN ON THE PATIO

FLANK STEAK TERIYAKI *
BAKED STUFFED POTATOES *
SPINACH SALAD WITH HOT DRESSING *
PEACHES WITH SHERRY CREAM *
CALIFORNIA STRAWBERRIES *

Another meat entree suited for finishing on the grill. Does equally well under the broiler if June's fickle weather turns out to be inhospitable.

FLANK STEAK TERIYAKI

¾ cup cooking oil
¼ cup soy sauce
¼ cup honey
2 tablespoons vinegar
2 tablespoons green onion (minced)
1 large clove garlic (crushed)
1½ teaspoons ginger
1 flank steak

Combine marinade ingredients and pour over steak. Marinate four hours or more. Barbeque, either on an outdoor grill or in the oven, using marinade for sauce. Carve on the diagonal grain.

BAKED STUFFED POTATOES

4 baked potatoes
4 tablespoons butter
½ teaspoon freshly ground pepper
1 teaspoon salt
4 tablespoons grated Cheddar cheese
2 tablespoons milk
grated Parmesan cheese

Cut hot baked potatoes in half, and scoop out potato into a warm bowl. Blend well with seasonings, cheese and milk. Return to potato shells and sprinkle with Parmesan cheese. Bake in 375° oven for about 15 minutes.

SPINACH SALAD WITH HOT DRESSING

¼ cup vinegar
½ cup water
1 cup sugar
2 eggs (beaten)
spinach (washed and torn into bite-sized pieces)
6 slices bacon (cooked and crumbled)
5-6 green onions (sliced)
2 hard cooked eggs (sliced)

Boil vinegar, water, and sugar until sugar is dissolved. Beat eggs until frothy, and add carefully to hot mixture. Pour over remaining ingredients while hot. Serve hot.

PEACHES WITH SHERRY CREAM

3-4 large fresh peaches
¾ cup sugar
2 cups water
1 teaspoon vanilla
2 egg yolks
¼ teaspoon salt
¾ cup sifted powdered sugar
⅓ cup sherry
½ pint (1 cup) whipping cream
nutmeg

Peel peaches, cut in half and remove pits. Bring sugar and water to boil, add peaches and simmer 5-10 minutes. Add vanilla, chill until ready to serve. Beat egg yolks with salt until thick. Add powdered sugar and beat until lemon colored. Whip cream until stiff, fold into egg mixture, add sherry. Spoon over peaches. Sprinkle with nutmeg.

CALIFORNIA STRAWBERRIES

1 pint strawberries with hulls
1 cup sour cream
½ cup brown sugar

Wash strawberries and place in large bowl. Serve as a Fondue.

Dip strawberries in sour cream and then dip in brown sugar.

Fun to do and delicious!

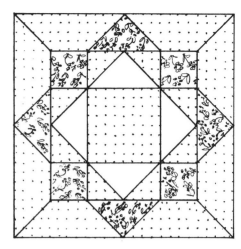

BRIDE'S CHOICE
Pattern on page 118

Ladies, to this advice give heed—
In controlling men:
If at first you don't succeed,
Why, cry, cry again.

Author Unknown

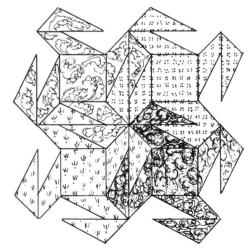

CRAB©
Pattern on page 119

A WEDDING SUPPER

CRAB BISQUE *

SIPPETS *

CRUDITES

SPONGE CAKE *

FRESH STRAWBERRIES

Not the type of menu suitable for a big affair, but perfect for an intimate supper to entertain the Bride and Groom and a few special friends. It could even be ideal for a shower luncheon.

CRAB BISQUE

½ cup finely shredded carrot
¼ cup finely chopped onion
¼ cup butter
3 tablespoons flour
2 cups chicken stock (canned is fine)
1 quart half and half cream
1 teaspoon salt
¼ cup sherry
2 cups crab meat (or any cooked seafood or combination)
dash cayenne
freshly ground black pepper
½ bunch of watercress (finely chopped)

Lightly saute carrot and onion in butter but do not brown. Stir flour into butter mixture, add chicken stock and cook until thickened. Add half and half, salt, sherry, and crab meat. Heat but do not allow to boil. Add cayenne, pepper and watercress. Serve very hot.

SIPPETS

Trim crust from sliced bread then cut into sticks, or any shape you wish (a fish cookie cutter is fine). Place on baking sheet and toast in 350° oven until lightly brown and crisp.

SPONGE CAKE

6 eggs
1¾ cups flour
1½ cups sugar
1 teaspoon vanilla
6 tablespoons water

Separate eggs. Beat whites until frothy, gradually add ¾ cup of the sugar and continue to beat until whites are stiff.

Beat yolks with remainder of the sugar (1 cup) until thick and lemon color. Stir in water and vanilla. Fold yolk mixture into whites only until blended. Pour into ungreased tube pan. Bake in 350° oven for 40 minutes. Turn pan upside-down to cool.

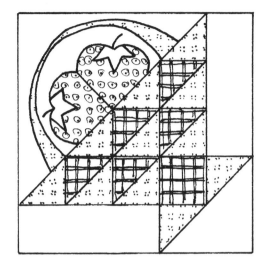

STRAWBERRY BASKET©
Pattern on page 120

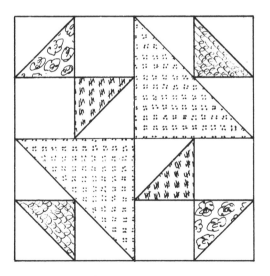

OLD MAID'S PUZZLE
Pattern on page 122

JULY

SUNDAY	MONDAY	TUESDAY	WEDNESDAY	THURSDAY	FRIDAY	SATURDAY
				Don't forget the real meaning of July the fourth.		
 Poseidon's Star©			Commenced July 8th 1872 Finished September 24th 1872 by E.B.B. in her 91st year Inscription on a Double Irish Chain quilt.		**July 4th**	
	He who pitches too high won't get through his song. German Proverb		 **Stars and Stripes**		Make a collection of various pieces of fabric as you travel from place to place on your vacation. Even the kids might like to help in the selection. These fabric "souvenirs" will provide vacation memories.	
	 Fireworks©			ONE, TWO, Whatever you do, Start it well, And carry it through.		

A QUILTER'S SHOPPING LIST

Cabbage and crackers,
two spools of thread,
a can of soup,
a loaf of sliced bread.

A few fat quarters
(one green for the trees)
two blue, one brown,
rice and swiss cheese.

Potatoes, corn flakes,
a new blade for my cutter.
Butterscotch pudding,
a quilt batt and butter.

Chuck roast, yogurt,
canned tomatoes and beans,
can't think of its name—
a thing to rip seams.

Mushrooms and soap,
lettuce (two heads),
Scraps for my quilt
of colorfast reds.

Plastic for templates,
Sardines (four tins),
cottage cheese, a melon,
a large box of pins.

A green pepper or two,
pretzels and chips.
Try the new quilt shop
for good fabric snips.

CHEERS FOR CHICKEN

CHEESY CHICKEN *

ITALIAN BEAN TOSS *

CREOLE RICE *

ROLLS

FROZEN TROPICAL FRUIT MOLD*

In the cool, cool, cool of the morning, fix the chicken, salad and dessert. You can even saute the vegetables for the rice at the same time. Meal-time preparation will be minimal. Great for entertaining. Spend the afternoon in an air-conditioned quilt shop.

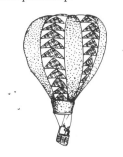

CHEESY CHICKEN

3 whole chicken breasts (skinned and split)
1 clove garlic (minced)
½ cup melted butter
½ cup fine dry bread crumbs
¼ cup finely grated sharp Cheddar cheese
2 tablespoons grated Parmesan cheese
Salt and pepper

Add garlic to melted butter and let stand 20 minutes. Mix together bread crumbs and cheese. Salt and pepper the chicken and dip in melted butter, then into crumb mixture.

Place in 9 x 13-in. dish. Pour remaining butter over chicken.

Bake uncovered in 350° oven for 45 minutes. Serves 6

ITALIAN BEAN TOSS

2-9 ounce packages frozen Italian green beans
½ cup mayonnaise
2 tablespoons grated Parmesan cheese
1 tablespoon chopped pimento
1 teaspoon salt
¼ teaspoon curry powder

Cook beans, drain and chill. Combine in mixing bowl mayonnaise, cheese, pimento, salt, and curry powder. Add beans, toss and chill. Serves 6-8

CREOLE RICE

1 cup uncooked rice
2 fresh tomatoes (peeled and chopped)
½ pound fresh mushrooms (sliced)
½ cup onion (chopped)
½ cup green pepper (chopped)
¼ cup butter
1 teaspoon salt
¼ teaspoon pepper
3 cups chicken broth

Saute rice, tomatoes, mushrooms, onion, and pepper in butter for 8 to 10 minutes. Add broth and seasonings. Cover and cook on low heat for 30 minutes or until rice is cooked.
Serves 6-8

FROZEN TROPICAL FRUIT MOLD

2 cups sour cream
4½ ounces frozen whipped dessert topping
1 cup sugar
4 tablespoons lemon juice
2 teaspoons vanilla
2 cans crushed pineapple (13 ounces each) (drained)
4 medium bananas (sliced)
1 jar maraschino cherries (4 ounces) (cut up)

Combine all ingredients, put into a decorative mold.

Freeze. Unmold to serve.

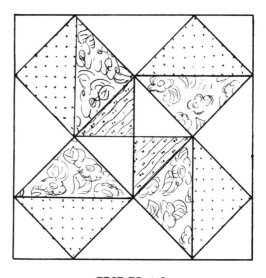

JULY 4th
Pattern on page 123

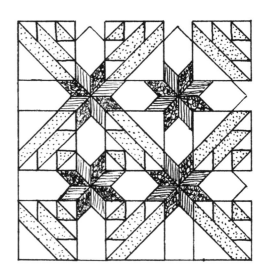

POSEIDON'S STAR©
Pattern on page 122

A SUMMERTIME LUNCHEON WITH A FRENCH FLAVOR

BLUEBERRY SOUP *

SALAD NICOISE *

HERBED TOMATO CHEESE BREAD *

POT DE CREME *

If you're short on time (or energy) serve French bread or hard rolls instead of the Herbed Tomato Cheese Bread. The Herbed Tomato Cheese Bread, however, can stand on its own for a light summertime treat. Serve wedges for an hors d'oeuvre on the patio before a barbecue.

BLUEBERRY SOUP

4 cups blueberries (fresh or frozen)
4 cups lemonade
⅓ cup honey
1 stick cinnamon
2 tablespoons lemon juice

Simmer all together (except lemon juice) for 15 minutes. Puree in blender and add lemon juice. Chill and serve with a spoonful of sour cream or yogurt, and a sprinkle of ground cinnamon.

SALAD NICOISE

Fill a large glass bowl with torn greens (preferably romaine and leaf lettuces). Add sliced onion, wedges of tomatoes, black olives, drained tuna and slices of hard cooked egg.

Serve with the following dressing:

VINAIGRETTE

½ onion (chopped)
1 clove garlic (minced)
½ cup salad oil (part olive)
¼ cup red wine vinegar
1 teaspoon prepared mustard
½ teaspoon salt
¼ teaspoon pepper

Combine all ingredients. Let stand a few minutes for flavors to blend.

HERBED TOMATO CHEESE BREAD

Topping:

1 medium onion (minced)
2 tablespoons butter
¾ cup sour cream
⅓ cup mayonnaise
¾ teaspoon salt
¼ teaspoon pepper
4 ounce grated Cheddar cheese (about 1 cup)
¼ teaspoon oregano
pinch of sage
fresh ripe tomatoes (sliced)

Saute onion in butter until tender. Combine onion with all other topping ingredients except tomatoes.

Bread:

⅔ cup milk
2 cups Bisquick

Stir milk into Bisquick to make a soft dough. Turn dough onto a well-floured board and knead lightly 10-12 strokes. Pat dough over bottom of a buttered 9 x 13 baking dish, pushing dough up sides to form a shallow rim. Arrange tomato slices over dough. Spoon on sour cream topping and sprinkle with paprika.

Bake in a 400° oven for 20-25 minutes. Let stand 10 minutes before cutting. Serves 12

POT DE CREME

1 package (6 ounces) chocolate chips or 1 cup
2 tablespoons sugar
1 egg
pinch salt
1 teaspoon vanilla
¾ cup milk

Place all ingredients (except milk) in blender. Heat milk just to boiling. Add milk to blender and blend 1 minute. Immediately pour into 6 serving dishes. Chill. Serve with whipped cream. For an added touch, flavor pot de creme with orange liquor or rum to taste. Add to blender before the hot milk. Serves 6

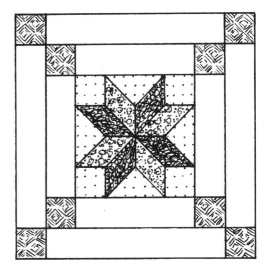

STARS AND STRIPES FOREVER
Pattern on page 123

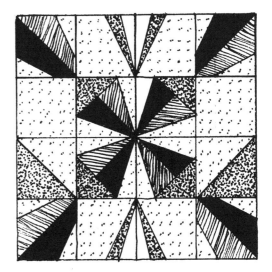

FIREWORKS©
Pattern on page 126

AUGUST

SUNDAY	MONDAY	TUESDAY	WEDNESDAY	THURSDAY	FRIDAY	SATURDAY
		Quilters don't quit . . . they just go to pieces.				
			Sand Castles©			
	Milky Way				Dog days of summer.	**Scottie Dog©**
		Build on, and make thy castles high and fair, Rising and reaching upward to the skies. Longfellow				
He that is overcautious will accomplish little. *Wilhelm Tell* Schiller						**Corn and Beans**

47

DOGGIE COOKIES

1 package dry yeast
¼ cup lukewarm water
1 cup lukewarm
   chicken broth
2 tablespoons molasses
1¾-2 cups all-purpose
   flour
1½ cups whole wheat
   flour

1 cup cracked wheat
½ cup corn meal
½ cup dry milk powder
2 teaspoons garlic powder

Glaze:
1 beaten egg
1 tablespoon milk

Dissolve yeast in warm water. Stir all ingredients together, knead and roll ⅜″ to ½″ thick. Cut into desired shapes. Place on ungreased cookie sheets. Brush with glaze. Bake at 300° for 45 minutes. Turn oven off and let dry overnight.

Your doggie will be able to tolerate those long wearisome dog days with an occasional "homemade" dog cookie.

SUMMER PICNIC WITH FRIENDS

BAKED HAM WITH GLAZES *
BAKED LIMAS *
GERMAN POTATO SALAD *
LAYERED SALAD *
ZELA'S ICE CREAM *
JUMBO RAISIN COOKIES *
APRICOT MERINGUE BARS *

You'll find a lot of bacon here, but it is indispensible to these recipes. You may want to choose some alternative dishes. All the recipes are great picnic fare, so be sure to try them on some occasion.

HAM GLAZES

For added flavor and color, spread one of the following glazes on your ham during the last 30 minutes of heating time:

Cherry Glaze:

1 cup cherry jelly or preserves
2 tablespoons lemon juice
1 teaspoon cinnamon
¼ teaspoon allspice

Mix ingredients in a pan. Heat, stirring constantly, until jelly dissolves.

Honey Glaze:

½ cup honey
¼ cup orange juice
2 tablespoons vinegar
2 teaspoons cornstarch

Combine ingredients. Heat, stirring constantly, until slightly thickened. (Note: maple syrup may be substituted for honey).

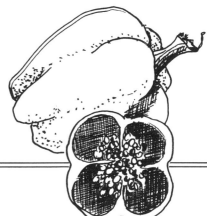

BAKED LIMAS

2 cans Seaside limas (drained) (16 ounces each)
6 slices bacon
1 medium onion (chopped)
½ green pepper (chopped)
⅓ bottle chili sauce
¾ cup brown sugar

Fry bacon and remove from pan, fry onions and pepper in bacon fat until soft. Combine limas, onion, pepper, chili sauce, and sugar. Add crumbled bacon and mix.

Bake uncovered in 300° oven for 1 hour. Serves 6

GERMAN POTATO SALAD

3 or 4 medium potatoes (cooked and sliced, keep hot)
6 slices cooked bacon (the best is from a country butcher shop)
½ cup sliced celery
3 tablespoons chopped onion
1 small clove garlic (minced)
1 tablespoon cornstarch
½ cup water
¼ cup vinegar
1 tablespoon sugar
1 teaspoon prepared mustard
salt and pepper to taste

Combine cornstarch, water, vinegar, and sugar. Cook until thickened, add mustard, salt and pepper. Stir in potatoes, onions, celery and garlic. Sprinkle with crumbled bacon. Serve warm. This can be served cold also. Serves 6

LAYERED OVERNIGHT LETTUCE SALAD

1½ heads lettuce
2 cups fresh mushrooms (sliced)
2 cups red onions (sliced)
1 cup mayonnaise
1 cup sour cream
1 tablespoon sugar
1 teaspoon prepared mustard
1 cup grated Parmesan cheese
4 slices bacon (cooked crisp and crumbled)

Cut lettuce in wedges and place cut side down in large bowl. Top with mushrooms, then onions. Combine mayonnaise, sugar, sour cream, and mustard. Spread over top of vegetables, being sure to seal to edge of dish. Sprinkle with Parmesan cheese. Cover with plastic wrap and refrigerate for 24 hours. Before serving, sprinkle with bacon. Serves 6 to 8

He who works with his hands is a laborer;
He who works with his head and his hands
* is a craftsman;*
He who works with his head and his hands
* and his heart is an artist.*

Author Unknown

SAND CASTLES©
Pattern on page 128

MILKY WAY
Pattern on page 129

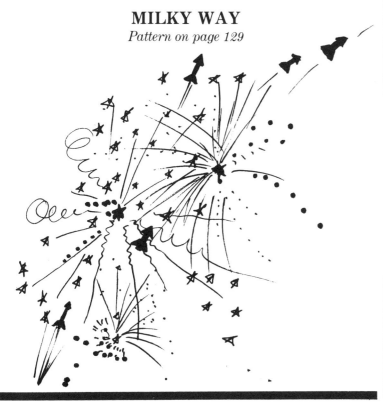

ZELA'S HOMEMADE ICE CREAM

3 cups milk
1½ cups sugar
4 tablespoons flour
salt
4 eggs or 6 egg yolks
3 teaspoons vanilla
3 cups heavy cream

Scald milk, add sugar and flour. Stir over heat until thickened. Simmer 10 minutes. Beat eggs slightly and add a small amount of hot milk to egg, then stir into milk. Cook for 1 minute. Cool. Add cream and vanilla.

Freeze according to instructions accompanying ice cream freezer. Serves 8

JUMBO RAISIN COOKIES

1 cup water
2 cups raisins
1 cup shortening
2 cups sugar
3 eggs
1 teaspoon vanilla
1 cup nuts (chopped)

4 cups flour
1 teaspoon baking powder
1 teaspoon baking soda
1½ teaspoons cinnamon
¼ teaspoon nutmeg
¼ teaspoon allspice

Cook raisins in water for five minutes. Allow to cool. *Do not drain.*

Cream shortening and sugar, add eggs and vanilla, beat well. Sift dry ingredients together and add to creamed mixture along with raisins and their liquid. Add nuts if desired.

Drop by spoonful onto greased cookie sheet.

Bake in 400° oven for 12-15 minutes. Makes 60 cookies

APRICOT MERINGUE BARS

1 cup margarine
½ cup sugar
½ teaspoon vanilla
2 cups sifted flour
1 jar apricot preserves (12 ounces)
2 egg whites
½ teaspoon almond extract
1 cup confectioner's sugar
¼ cup almonds (sliced)

Cream margarine, sugar and vanilla until light and fluffy. Add flour and mix thoroughly. Spread in 9 x 13-inch pan, bake at 350° for 15 minutes. Cool thoroughly. Spread preserves over crust gently. Beat egg whites and extract slightly, using electric mixer. Beat in sugar gradually; mixture acts as a glaze and is thin. Spread over preserves carefully, then top with nuts. Bake at 400° for 20 minutes, or until delicately browned. Cut in squares to serve.

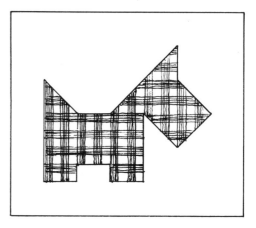

SCOTTIE DOG©
Pattern on page 130

GARDEN BONANZA

CORN FRITTERS *

MARINATED VEGGIES *

ZUCCHINI BREAD *

FRESH SLICED PEACHES WITH PUREE

OF RASPBERRY TOPPING

The garden scores with this menu, bounteous with summer's vegetables. Add a meat entree if you want—roast chicken, cheeseburgers, grilled fish. . .

CORN FRITTERS

2 cups fresh corn
2 egg yolks (beaten)
4 tablespoons flour
½ teaspoon salt
freshly ground pepper to taste
2 egg whites
shortening (about ¼-inch deep)

Combine corn, egg yolks, flour, salt and pepper. Beat egg whites, and gently fold into corn mixture. Drop by tablespoonsful into hot shortening and fry until nicely browned on both sides. Serves 6

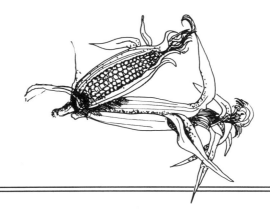

MARINATED VEGGIES

3 red, ripe tomatoes (peeled and cut into wedges)
1 medium onion (sliced)
1 medium green pepper (sliced)
1 cucumber (thinly sliced)
1 cup Italian salad dressing

Place vegetables in a dish. Pour dressing over and toss lightly. Let stand a while before serving.

ZUCCHINI BREAD

3 eggs
1 cup safflower oil
1½ cups sugar
2 cups grated zucchini (don't drain)
2½ cups flour
1 teaspoon baking powder
¾ teaspoon baking soda
2 teaspoons cinnamon
1 cup raisins
1 cup chopped nuts

Beat eggs slightly in large bowl. Stir in oil, zucchini and sugar. Mix dry ingredients and stir into egg mixture. Add in nuts and raisins. Pour into 3 small greased and floured loaf pans.

Bake in 375° oven for 45 minutes.

We may live without poetry, music
   and art;
We may live without conscience, and
   live without heart;
We may live without friends; we may
   live without books;
But civilized man cannot live without
   cooks.

Lucille
Owen Meredith

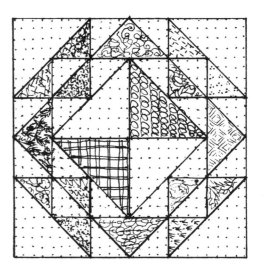

CORN AND BEANS
Pattern on page 132

SEPTEMBER

SUNDAY	MONDAY	TUESDAY	WEDNESDAY	THURSDAY	FRIDAY	SATURDAY
			Don't forget to send a quilt along to college so your son or daughter will remember home, hearth, and mother, not to mention your phone number.	**Schoolhouse**		
Migrating Hawks©			Imagine the reaction if a quilter were finger-printed!	**Allentown Fair**	Many things difficult to design prove easy to perform. Samuel Johnson	
	From a 1930 diary from Upper Frederick Township, Montgomery County: September 2, Tuesday: Put quilt in a frame. September 5, Friday: Finished quilt. We will assume that the writer of this diary knotted rather than quilted the quilt, since the diary also states that during this time she also canned three baskets of peaches.					

THE QUILTING

"It has no golden value—
    That simple, patchwork spread;
Its squares, in homely fashion,
    Set in with green and red;
But in those faded pieces,
    For me are shining bright,
Oh! many a summer morning
    And many a winter night."

From An Anonymous Scrapbook
Olden Times: or, Pennsylvania
Rural Life Some Fifty Years Ago
        H. L. Fisher, 1888

SOUP FOR SUPPER

*FRIED TOMATO SOUP ***
*RYE SOFT PRETZELS ***
*TURNIP SLAW ***
RED GRAPES
SLICED CHEDDAR CHEESE
*RICE PUDDING ***

Don't be misled—the soup is not really fried. Fresh sliced tomatoes are lightly sauteed before making them into soup to give it a taste different from the usual. The base (without the milk) freezes well so you can enjoy the soup out of season. Make the pretzels to eat as a snack too, with cheese and chunks of "ring bologna," (a Pennsylvania Dutch smoked ready-to-eat sausage) while watching the big game or quilting. Use toothpicks and you can snack neatly.

FRIED TOMATO SOUP

4-5 large tomatoes (skinned and sliced)
4 tablespoons flour
2 tablespoons sugar
1½ teaspoons salt
⅛ teaspoon pepper
3 tablespoons margarine
milk

Combine flour, sugar, salt and pepper. Coat tomato slices with this mixture. Brown tomatoes in margarine. Simmer until soft. Process browned tomatoes in blender or food processor until smooth. Add equal amount of milk and heat thoroughly.

Concentrate can be frozen; do not add milk until ready to serve. Serves 4

RYE SOFT PRETZELS

1 package active dry yeast
1½ cups warm water
1 tablespoon molasses
1 teaspoon salt
2 cups rye flour
2-2¾ cups whole wheat flour
coarse salt

In mixing bowl, dissolve yeast in warm water. Add molasses and salt. Stir in flours until no longer sticky. Knead until smooth, about 5 minutes. Cut into 12 portions, roll each into a rope 15 inches long. Shape into pretzels, place on greased baking sheet. Moisten lightly with water, sprinkle with coarse salt.

Bake in 425° oven for 20 minutes or until browned.

Serve with mustard if desired. Makes 12

TURNIP SLAW

6 medium sized turnips
⅔ cup sour cream
2 tablespoons vinegar
2 tablespoons sugar
1 teaspoon salt
1 tablespoon parsley (chopped)

Pare and shred raw turnips. Pour over them a dressing made by combining sugar, salt, vinegar, and sour cream. Garnish with parsley. Serves 6

RICE PUDDING

2 cups milk
1 tablespoon butter
⅓ cup sugar
½ cup raisins
nutmeg to taste
1 cup rice (cooked al dente)
1 egg
1 teaspoon vanilla

Combine all ingredients except egg and vanilla in a saucepan. Simmer over low heat stirring constantly until reduced by half. This takes about 20 minutes. Remove from heat. Beat egg in a bowl, add some of the hot rice mixture and blend well. Add this to saucepan and allow to cook a few minutes. Add vanilla. Serves 4-5

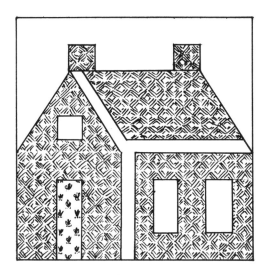

SCHOOLHOUSE
Pattern on page 133

SEPTEMBER SALAD

*HOT TOMATO JUICE COCKTAIL **
*ROYAL REUBEN SALAD **
CRACKERS OR RYE BREAD STICKS
*CHEESE PIE **
OR
*APPLE CRISP **

Hot Tomato Juice Cocktail is just the thing to add a bit of warmth to a salad meal, especially if September's winds blow suddenly cold. Try some crushed pineapple as a topping on the Cheese Pie. If you've opted for the Apple Crisp, you might like to omit the nuts and serve with butter pecan ice cream. Yum!

HOT TOMATO JUICE COCKTAIL

1 can tomato juice cocktail (46 ounces)
1 can beef broth (15 ounces)
1 tablespoon Worcestershire Sauce
1 teaspoon Tabasco sauce
¼ cup lemon juice

Heat thoroughly, but do not boil.

ROYAL REUBEN SALAD

6 cups assorted lettuces
1 small can sauerkraut (rinsed and drained)
1 cup cubed Swiss cheese
1 cup rye croutons
1½ cups cubed corned beef
½ cup Thousand Island salad dressing
½ teaspoon caraway seeds

Combine all ingredients in large bowl. Add croutons just before serving. Serves 6

CHEESE PIE

2-8-inch pie shells (unbaked)
1 pound cottage cheese (whipped)
4 eggs-beat whites separately
¼ teaspoon salt
1½ cups sugar
3 tablespoons flour
1 large can evaporated milk
1½ cups milk
1 teaspoon vanilla

Beat egg yolks, add cheese, salt, sugar, flour, and evaporated milk until blended. Beat egg whites until stiff. Add to egg mixture. Add milk and vanilla. Pour into pie shells.

Bake in 425° oven for 10 minutes. Reduce heat to 350° and bake an additional 30 minutes. Makes 2-8″ pies

APPLE CRISP

Filling:

5 cups apples (cored, pared and sliced)
¼ cup sugar
1 tablespoon water
½ teaspoon ground cinnamon
⅛ teaspoon ground allspice

Combine and spread in a greased 8 x 8-inch pan.

Topping:

½ cup packed brown sugar
½ cup flour
¼ cup rolled oats
¼ cup wheat germ
¼ cup chopped walnuts
½ teaspoon ground cinnamon
⅛ teaspoon ground allspice
6 tablespoons butter or margarine (softened)

In medium bowl combine all ingredients except butter. Cut in butter. Sprinkle over apple mixture.

Bake in 350° oven for 45 minutes or until top is browned and filling is bubbly. Serves 6-8

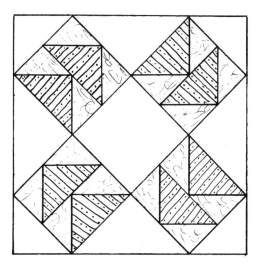

MIGRATING HAWKS©
Pattern on page 134

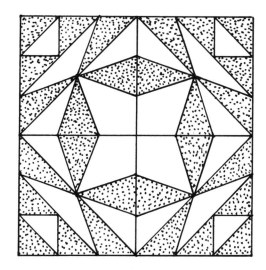

ALLENTOWN FAIR
Pattern on page 135

OCTOBER

SUNDAY	MONDAY	TUESDAY	WEDNESDAY	THURSDAY	FRIDAY	SATURDAY
			Don't ever shop for fabric on an empty stomach. Wait until after lunch so you won't have to hurry.		A handful of patience is worth more than a bushel of brains. Dutch Proverb	
	Wildflower Meadows©					**Canada Goose Tracks**
			Plan Christmas baking early. Make a separate shopping list with only these items. Begin in October and buy some of the expensive items each week so your budget won't go bang in December.			
	Oak Leaf and Reel				Send your kids out as Patchwork goblins. Sew all your fabric uglies into a Halloween costume.	**Morticia's Attic©**

61

A QUILTER IS ONE WHO:

— sneaks off to the local quilt shop three times a day

— quilts until her fingers are too sore to peel potatoes for supper

— brings fabric home in assorted small packages so it won't look like so much

— has blocks all over the bed, the table and the floor

— has fabric stored under beds, in suitcases, in the garage, and in boxes marked "Books"

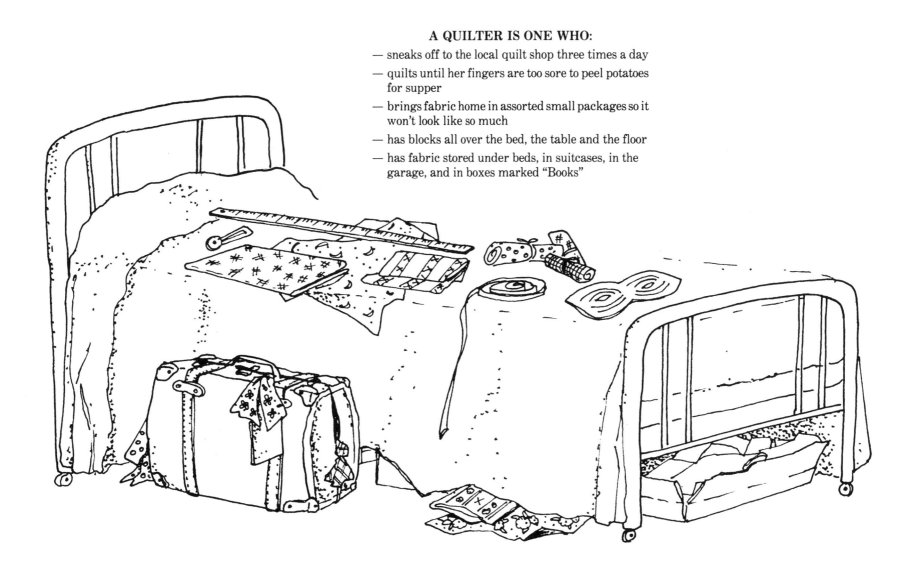

COLUMBUS DAY DINNER

*ROMAN HOLIDAY ***

TOSSED GREEN SALAD

OR

FRESH GREEN VEGETABLE

GARLIC BREAD

*FROSTY FRUIT DESSERT ***

A perfect menu for supper on quilt club meeting day. Mix the casserole in the morning and let the flavors blend all day while you blend the colors of your present project.

We do not what we ought;
What we ought not, we do;
And lean upon the thought
That Chance will bring us through.
                              Matthew Arnold

ROMAN HOLIDAY

1 onion (chopped)
1 pound hamburger
salt and pepper to taste
1 egg (beaten)
2 cups of cooked spaghetti (al dente)
¾ cup grated Parmesan cheese
1½ cups of canned chopped tomatoes or tomato juice
1 can tomato paste (6 ounces)

Brown meat and onion, remove from heat and add egg. Set aside. Mix tomatoes or juice with tomato paste. Set aside. Grease 1½ quart casserole. Place a small amount of tomato mixture in bottom, then spaghetti, meat, tomatoes. Repeat layers ending with a third layer of spaghetti on top (3 layers of spaghetti and 2 layers of meat). Top with remaining tomato mixture and ¾ cup Parmesan cheese.

Cover and bake in 350° oven for 35 minutes. Remove lid and bake for 10 minutes to brown cheese. Serves 3-4

FROSTY FRUIT DESSERT

1 cup miniature marshmallows
1 medium can pineapple crushed with juice
1 medium can sliced peaches (drained)
1 small can mandarin orange slices (drained)
fresh grapes (cut in half and remove seeds)
cherries (fresh or frozen)
8-12 ounces of Cool Whip
2 tablespoons mayonnaise
walnuts

Combine fruits. Mix mayonnaise into Cool Whip and blend into fruits. Top with walnuts.
Serves 6-8

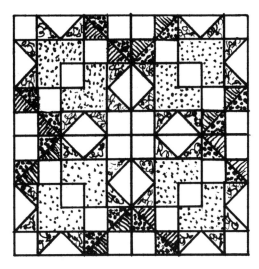

WILDFLOWER MEADOWS©
Pattern on page 137

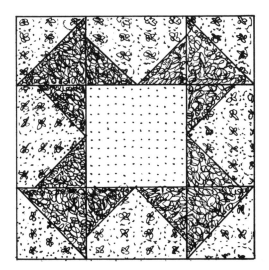

CANADA GOOSE TRACKS
Pattern on page 138

AUTUMN SURPRISE

AUTUMN SOUP *
SLICED FRESH APPLES & CHEESE
LEMON BREAD *
UPSIDE DOWN DATE PUDDING *

A "souper" supper for a cold night. Don't tell anyone the ingredients in the soup until they've eaten it. They won't believe they've eaten squash. The Lemon Bread is a fine little something to serve with a cup of tea—anytime.

It is a token of healthy and gentle characteristics, when women of high thoughts and accomplishments love to sew; especially as they are never more at home with their own hearts than while so occupied.

Nathaniel Hawthorne

AUTUMN SOUP

½ cup chopped leeks
½ cup chopped onion
½ cup chopped celery
2 large apples (peeled, cored, and finely chopped)
¼ cup butter
2 tablespoons flour
7 cups chicken or turkey stock
4 cups of butternut squash (peeled and diced)
1 teaspoon thyme
½ teaspoon sage
¼ teaspoon turmeric
¼ teaspoon rosemary
pinch of nutmeg
1 teaspoon salt
pinch of pepper
1 cup apple cider
1 quart half and half
1 cup grated cheese
croutons

In a large kettle, saute leeks, onion, celery and apple in butter until tender. Stir in flour and cook a few minutes. Add stock and simmer for 10 minutes. Then add squash and cook until squash is tender. Add remaining ingredients except cider and half and half. Simmer 5 minutes. Stir in cider and half and half and heat thoroughly. Remove from heat and stir in cheese. Garnish with croutons.

Makes about 1 gallon. If desired, puree or strain before adding cheese.

LEMON BREAD

1 cup sugar
¼ cup plain shortening
¼ cup butter flavor shortening
2 eggs
½ cup milk
grated rind of one lemon

1½ cup flour
1 teaspoon baking powder
½ teaspoon salt
¼ cup white sugar
3 tablespoons lemon juice

Cream shortening and sugar until light and fluffy. Add eggs, milk, and rind, then add flour sifted with salt and baking powder. Pour batter into greased and floured loaf pan.

Bake for one hour at 350°. Remove from pan. While still warm, brush with the ¼ cup sugar and the 3 tablespoons lemon juice, mixed, on top and sides. Allow to cool before cutting.

UPSIDE DOWN DATE PUDDING

1 cup pitted dates
2 tablespoons butter
1 cup boiling water
1 egg
1½ cup flour
½ cup sugar
½ cup brown sugar

½ cup brown sugar
1 teaspoon soda
½ teaspoon baking powder
½ teaspoon salt
½ cup broken walnuts
1½ cups brown sugar
1½ cups boiling water

Snip dates into a 9-inch round or square baking dish. Add butter. Pour 1 cup boiling water over dates and stir to melt butter and soften dates. Mix together egg, flour, sugar, ½ cup brown sugar, soda, baking powder, salt and walnuts until thoroughly blended. Smooth batter evenly over dates, and sprinkle with remaining brown sugar. Slowly pour 1½ cup boiling water over all.

Bake for 40 minutes in 350° oven. Serve warm with vanilla ice cream. Serves 6

OAK LEAF AND REEL
Pattern on page 139

MORTICIA'S ATTIC©
Pattern on page 140

NOVEMBER

SUNDAY	MONDAY	TUESDAY	WEDNESDAY	THURSDAY	FRIDAY	SATURDAY
				A politician thinks of the next election; a statesman, of the next generation. James Freeman Clarke		
	Vote early, put on a pot of soup, and you'll feel good about quilting all day.	**Election Game**				**Pilgrim's Journey©**
				Turkey Tracks		
Northeast Wind					Most people would succeed in small things if they were not troubled with great ambitions. *Driftwood* Longfellow	

For filling quilts, ordinary cotton batting may be used, but for quilts upon which very fine work is to be done, cotton sheet wadding is preferred because of its smoothness and lack of bulkiness. Oftentimes worn blankets may be very satisfactorily used as the filling for quilts.

Though comfortables have largely supplanted quilts, it is not unusual to find persons at the present time who make very beautiful patchwork quilts.

Quilt piecing has always been considered good as practice work for beginners in sewing because of the accuracy that is necessary in cutting and stitching.

Household Sewing, 1923

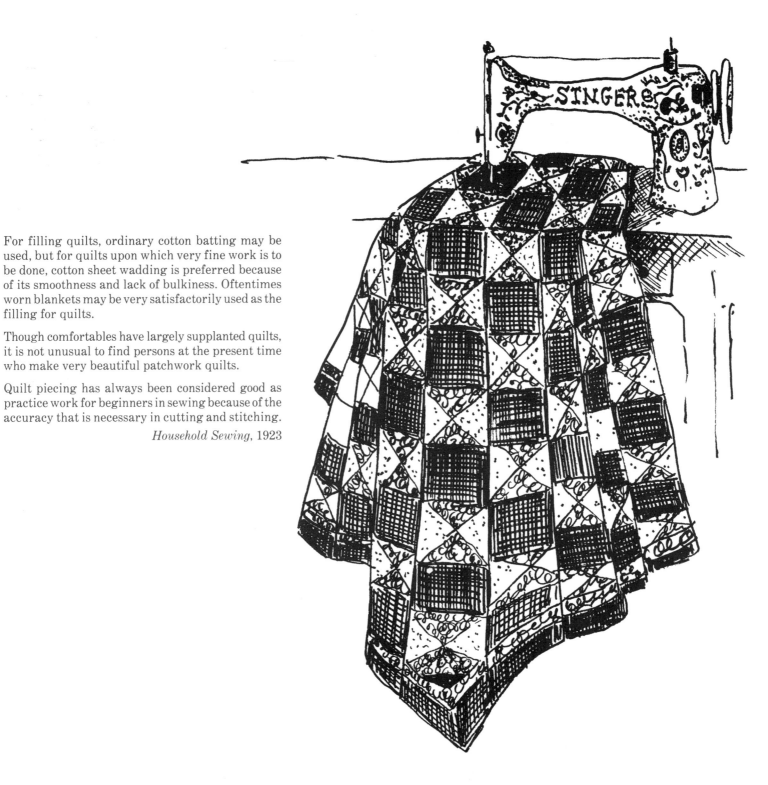

A GREAT
FALL SUPPER

CHICKEN PIE *

BROCCOLI SALAD *

PUMPKIN GINGER SNAP SQUARES *

Who doesn't love chicken pie? The dill weed in the crust sets this pie above the average. Pumpkin Ginger Snap Squares would be an easy dessert for Thanksgiving dinner in place of the traditional pie.

CHICKEN PIE

2½ cups cooked diced chicken
1 can cream of celery or cream of chicken soup
½ cup sliced celery
1 teaspoon bottled steak sauce or Worcestershire Sauce
3 medium potatoes (diced)
green pepper and mushrooms (optional)
½ teaspoon marjoram
dillweed
pastry for 9-inch pie dish

Combine soup, celery, potatoes, and steak sauce in saucepan. Simmer about 10 minutes. Turn into shallow baking dish. Add chicken. Prepare pastry. Add a liberal amount of dillweed to water when mixing pastry. Roll out pastry and place over baking dish. Cut opening in crust.

Bake for 20 minutes in 450° oven. Let stand 10 minutes before serving. Serves 4 to 6

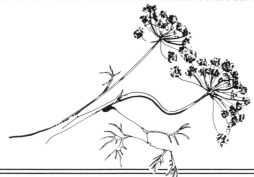

BROCCOLI SALAD

1 bunch fresh broccoli
1 cup raisins
4 navel oranges (peeled and sectioned)
½ red onion (sliced)
5 slices bacon (cooked and crumbled)
½ cup slivered almonds (toasted)

Dressing:

½ cup sugar
¾ cup mayonnaise
¼ cup white vinegar

Cut up raw broccoli into flowerettes, add raisins, sectioned oranges, onion, bacon, and almonds. Toss ingredients. Blend dressing ingredients in blender, add to salad.

PUMPKIN-GINGER SNAP SQUARES

1 pound pumpkin (16 ounces)
1 cup sugar
1 teaspoon salt
1 teaspoon ginger
1 teaspoon cinnamon
½ teaspoon nutmeg
1 cup chopped nuts
vanilla ice cream (½ gallon)
gingersnaps
whipped cream

Mix the first seven ingredients. Add ½ gallon vanilla ice cream. Line bottom of pan with ginger snaps. Cover with half of mixture. Add another layer of ginger snaps, then the remainder of mixture. Freeze. Garnish with whipped cream. Serves 12-16

A weapon that comes down as still
    As snow-flakes fall upon the sod,
But executes a freeman's will,
    As lightning does the will of God;
And from its force nor doors nor locks
    Can shield you—'tis the ballot-box.

A Word from a Petitioner
John Pierpont

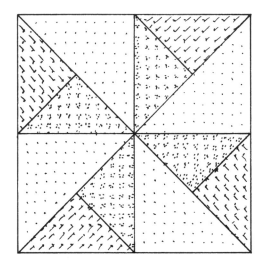

ELECTION GAME
Pattern on page 141

"SOUPER" SUNDAY SUPPER

---

*KIDNEY BEAN SOUP ***

*GRILLED CHEESE PIE ***

OR

*ONION PIE ***

*HEARTY GREEN SALAD ***

*RASPBERRY DELIGHT DESSERT ***

This soup is hefty, hot and hearty. You'll like the Grilled Cheese Pie so much you'll want to serve it for a simple and easy lunch anytime. To complicate your life, make the Onion Pie. It's more than worth the effort.

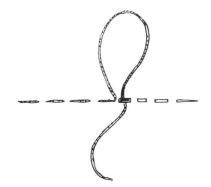

KIDNEY BEAN SOUP

1 pound sausage (½ sweet and ½ hot Italian)
2 cans kidney beans (16 ounce)
1 can crushed tomatoes (12 ounce)
1 quart water
1 large onion (chopped)
1 bay leaf
1½ teaspoons seasoned salt
½ teaspoon garlic salt
½ teaspoon thyme
⅛ teaspoon pepper
½ green pepper (chopped)
1 cup diced cooked potatoes

Remove casing from sausage and crumble or just cut sausage into slices. Brown slightly with onion. Combine remaining ingredients except potatoes and simmer one hour. Add potatoes and heat. Serves 8

GRILLED CHEESE PIE

1 egg
¾ cup flour
½ teaspoon salt
⅛ teaspoon pepper
1 cup milk
1 cup Munster cheese (shredded)

Combine egg, flour, salt, pepper, and half of the milk. Add remaining milk and blend. Stir in half of the cheese. Pour into a well-greased 8-inch pie pan.

Bake in 425° oven for 30 minutes. Sprinkle remaining cheese over top and return to oven just until cheese is melted (about 2 minutes).

ONION PIE

1-9″ pie crust
1 pound onions (not Spanish or Bermuda)
4 tablespoons butter
pinch of freshly grated nutmeg
pinch of salt and pepper
2 tablespoons flour
3 eggs
1½ cups heavy cream

Preheat oven to 425°. Peel and slice the onions. Melt the butter in a skillet, add the onions, and season with the nutmeg, salt and pepper. Gently saute over moderate heat until the onions are soft and pale yellow. Set aside. Combine flour and eggs and gradually add the cream. Add reserved onions and blend. Set aside.

Line a flan mold or 9-inch pie plate with rolled pastry. Add filling and bake in a 425° oven for 10 minutes. Reduce heat to 350° and continue to bake for 30 minutes. Serve warm. Serves 6-8

Modern invention has banished the spinning-wheel, and the same law of progress makes the woman of today a different woman from her grandmother.

Susan B. Anthony

PILGRIM'S JOURNEY©
Pattern on page 144

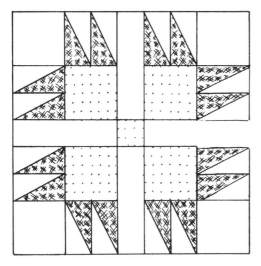

TURKEY TRACKS

Pattern on page 143

**To Keep Blue Calicoes
Bright and Fresh**
The first time they are washed, put them
in water with a cupful spirits of turpentine
to each pail of water. This will set the color,
and they will always look well.

Housekeeping in Old Virginia (1879)

HEARTY GREEN SALAD

1 head leaf lettuce (washed and drained)
1-6 ounce jar marinated artichoke hearts (drain, save oil)
½ cup pitted ripe olives (sliced)
croutons
Parmesan cheese

Dressing:

juice of ½ lemon
1 teaspoon dillweed
¼ cup olive oil
½ teaspoon salt
dash pepper
marinate from artichoke hearts

Tear lettuce into small pieces, cut olives and artichoke hearts into pieces and mix with
lettuce. Toss with dressing just before serving, add croutons and Parmesan cheese to taste.

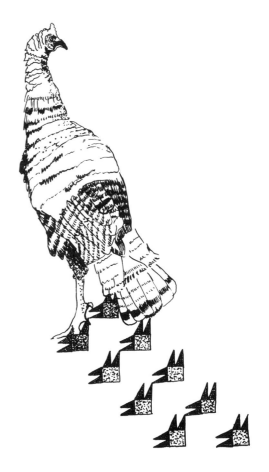

RASPBERRY DELIGHT DESSERT

1 package raspberry Jello (3-ounce)
1 cup hot water
1 cup vanilla ice cream
3 tablespoons orange juice
1 can crushed pineapple (9 ounce)
1 medium banana (sliced)
½ cup chopped pecans

Dissolve gelatin in hot water, mix in ice cream and orange juice until blended. Chill until partially set. Add fruit and nuts. Pour into 1 quart mold. Chill until set.

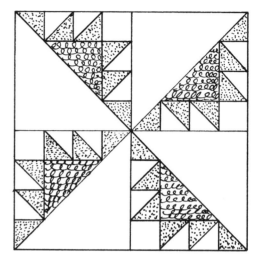

NORTH EAST WIND
Pattern on page 141

**About the only difference
between stumbling blocks
and stepping stones
is the way you use them.**

Bernard Meltzer

DECEMBER

SUNDAY	MONDAY	TUESDAY	WEDNESDAY	THURSDAY	FRIDAY	SATURDAY
		Pieced Teddy Bear©	Teddy Bears and Quilts have a lot in common— they both give warmth.		I like trees because they seem more resigned to the way they have to live than other things do. Willa Cather	
Evergreen Fir Tree			Bow Tie	Grandmother's Christmas Cactus		Star of Stars©
		Christmas itself may be called into question If carried so far it cre- ates indigestion. Ralph Bergengren				

I love the Christmas-tide, and yet,
  I notice this, each year I live;
I always like the gifts I get,
  But how I love the gifts I give!

A Thought
Carolyn Wells

OUR CHRISTMAS CARRY-IN

SHRIMP LAMAIZE *
PINEAPPLE CHEESE BALL *
ROAST PORK
CRANBERRY STUFFING *
BRUSSEL SPROUTS *
ASPARAGUS SUPREME *
CABBAGE RELISH *
CHOCOLATE MYSTERY CAKE *
FRUIT TORTE *

The Christmas meeting of the Variable Star Quilters is traditionally a carry-in biggie, with the hostess providing the entree, and it includes the works. This menu is made up of favorites from these occasions. Almost any meat could substitute, but a crown roast of pork is a spectacular presentation.

SHRIMP LAMAIZE

2 pounds shrimp (cooked and deveined)
1 pound crabmeat
1 pint mayonnaise
1 bottle chili sauce
½ cup India relish (drained)
3 hard boiled eggs (grated)
1 onion (finely grated)
1 teaspoon dry mustard

Stir eggs and onion into mayonnaise and chili sauce. Add drained India relish and dry mustard. Mix in shrimp and crabmeat. Serve with crackers.

PINEAPPLE CHEESE BALL

2 packages cream cheese (8 ounces each)
1 can crushed pineapple (drained) (8½ ounces)
2 cups chopped pecans
¼ cup chopped green pepper
2 tablespoons chopped onion
1 teaspoon salt

Let cheese soften at room temperature. Cream the cheese and stir in crushed pineapple. Add 1 cup pecans, green pepper, onion, and salt. Chill mixture. Form into a ball and roll in remaining pecans. Recipe makes two good size balls, and it freezes well.

CRANBERRY STUFFING

1½ cups raw cranberries (chopped)
3 tablespoons sugar
4 cups Pepperidge Farm Stuffing
1 teaspoon salt
¼ teaspoon thyme
¼ teaspoon nutmeg
¼ teaspoon sage
¼ cup chopped onion
1 clove garlic (mashed)

Combine cranberries and sugar, simmer until cooked. Add butter to melt. Stir into other ingredients and toss to blend. Use as a stuffing for a crown roast of pork or bake separately in a buttered casserole. Try as a stuffing for pork chops also.

BRUSSELS SPROUTS

2 bags brussels sprouts (24 ounces each)
¼ pound margarine
½ cup bread crumbs
⅔ cup English walnuts (chopped)
1 cup Cheddar cheese (cut into ¼-inch squares)

Cook sprouts according to directions on package. In small frying pan, melt margarine and add bread crumbs and walnuts. Saute until golden brown. Drain sprouts, put in baking dish with cheese on top of sprouts then bread crumbs and walnut mixture.

Bake in 350° oven for 15 minutes.

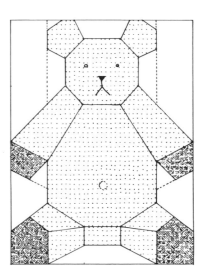

PIECED TEDDY BEAR©

Pattern on page 145

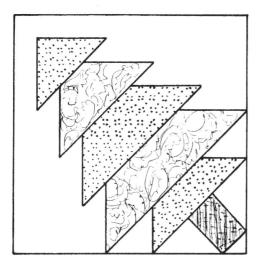

EVERGREEN FIR TREE

Pattern on page 146

ASPARAGUS SUPREME

2 cans asparagus spears (drained)
1 cup milk
3 tablespoons butter
Tabasco sauce
1 cup grated cheese
2 tablespoons flour
¼ teaspoon salt
3 hard cooked eggs (sliced)
½ cup toasted almonds (chopped)
buttered bread crumbs

Make a sauce from butter, flour, and milk. When thickened, add all the seasonings and the cheese and heat until blended. In a greased 9 x 13-inch casserole, make alternate layers of asparagus, sliced eggs, and almonds. Pour sauce over casserole and top with buttered bread crumbs. Bake, uncovered, at 350° for 30 minutes. Serves 6

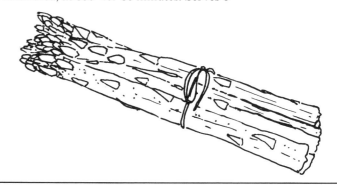

CABBAGE RELISH

⅔ cup water
¾ cup vinegar
1½ teaspoons salt
½ cup sugar
2 teaspoons celery seed
1 tablespoon mustard seed
6-7 cups shredded cabbage
1 green pepper (finely shredded)
1-4 ounce can pimento (finely shredded)
1 onion (finely chopped)
½ cup finely shredded carrot

Combine water, vinegar, salt, sugar and mustard seed in a saucepan. Bring to boil and simmer for 5 minutes. Cool. Pour over vegetables, toss, and chill.

CHOCOLATE MYSTERY CAKE

7 ounces semisweet chocolate or chocolate chips
¼ pound butter
1 cup sugar
7 eggs (separated)
whipped cream

Melt chocolate and butter in a saucepan over low heat. Gradually add sugar. Add egg yolks one at a time beating constantly. Beat at high speed for three minutes. Beat whites in a separate bowl until stiff. Fold into chocolate mixture. Pour ¾ of the batter into an ungreased spring form pan. Bake in 325° oven for 35 minutes. Remove from oven and allow to cool. It will fall. When cool, pour on remaining batter and chill. When ready to serve, remove from pan, garnish with whipped cream. Serves 8

FRUIT TORTE

1 cup sugar
½ cup butter
2 eggs
1 cup flour
1 teaspoon baking powder
¼ teaspoon salt
fruit
2 tablespoons lemon juice

Topping:

½ cup flour
¼ cup sugar
½ teaspoon cinnamon

Cream sugar and butter, add eggs and beat to blend well. Stir in remaining ingredients to make a dough. Press into a greased 9-inch springform pan. Spread entire top of dough with your choice of fresh or canned fruit. Peaches, apples, blueberries, raspberries, cherries. Sprinkle fruit with lemon juice, Combine topping ingredients and sprinkle on top of fruit. Bake at 350° for one hour.

GRANDMOTHER'S CHRISTMAS CACTUS
Pattern on page 148

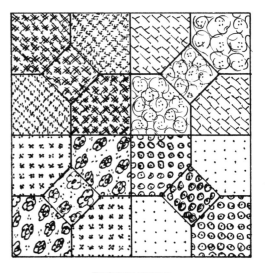

BOW TIE
Pattern on page 147

COMPANY FOR THE HOLIDAYS

FAVORITE PARTY CHICKEN *
LONG GRAIN AND WILD RICE CASSEROLE
STEAMED BROCCOLI
ORANGE AND ONION SALAD *
LEMON SPONGE PIE *

A menu suitable for a New Year's Eve buffet. Don't, however, serve chicken on New Year's day. One must eat pork (and preferably with sauerkraut) on the first day of the new year to assure oneself of success for the coming year. The pig roots forward while eating, while the chicken scratches for food and moves backward. Associating oneself with the more positive action is the best way to go, according to an old Pennsylvania Dutch custom.

FAVORITE PARTY CHICKEN

8 large chicken breasts (skinned and boned)
8 slices bacon
4 ounces chipped beef
2 cans undiluted Campbell's Mushroom soup
1 pint sour cream or soured half and half
¼ cup dry sherry

Wrap each chicken breast with a slice of bacon. Cover the bottom of a flat greased baking dish with chipped beef. Arrange chicken breasts on the chipped beef, making sure the ends of bacon are tucked under the chicken. Combine soup, sour cream and sherry. Pour half over the chicken. Reserve the other half. Refrigerate overnight or until ready to bake.

Bake uncovered in 275° oven for 3 hours.

Before serving, heat extra gravy and pour over chicken if needed. Serves 8

ORANGE AND ONION SALAD

1 medium red onion
2 large oranges
1 head romaine lettuce
½ cup almonds (toasted) (slivered)

Break romaine into salad bowl. Peel oranges and slice thin. Arrange orange slices, onion slices and almonds on romaine.

Dressing:

⅓ cup vegetable oil
1 tablespoon vinegar
¼ cup orange juice
pinch salt
½ teaspoon rosemary
freshly ground pepper

Combine and blend ingredients well. Pour over salad and toss just before serving. Serves 4-6

LEMON SPONGE PIE

1-9-inch pie shell (unbaked)
3 eggs (separated)
1 tablespoon lemon juice
1 teaspoon grated lemon rind
1 cup sugar
3 tablespoons flour
¼ teaspoon salt
1 tablespoon melted butter
1¼ cups milk

Beat egg yolks until thick and lemon colored. Add lemon juice and rind. Mix sugar, flour, salt and add to lemon mixture. Stir in butter and milk, fold in stiffly beaten egg whites. Pour into unbaked pie shell and bake in 450° oven for 10 minutes. Reduce heat to 350° and continue baking for 20-25 minutes longer until filling is set.

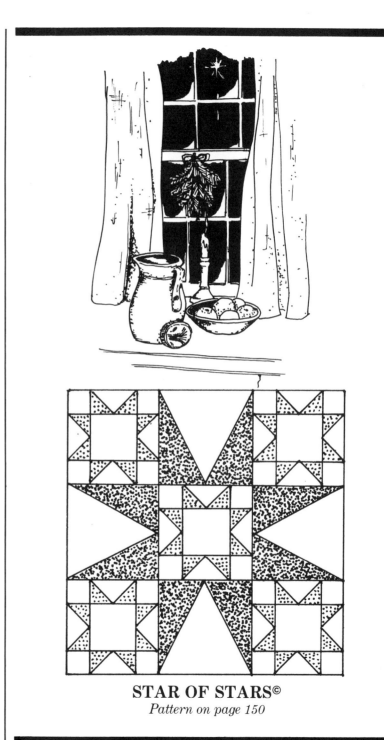

STAR OF STARS©
Pattern on page 150

OUR PENNSYLVANIA GERMAN HERITAGE

Since many of us have a Pennsylvania German background we feel it fitting to include some recipes for foods traditional to that culture.

Shoo Fly Pie is a well-known favorite as is the quilt block of the same name. Apeas cake is a lesser known cake. Both go well with a cup of coffee. Several other Pennsylvania German recipes are also given.

CHICKEN CORN SOUP

1 large stewing chicken
1 onion (cut up)
2 or 3 stalks celery (cut up)
Salt and pepper
2 cups cooked corn
1 cup noodles
2 hard cooked eggs (diced)
parsley

Cook chicken with onion and celery until tender, adding salt and pepper to taste. Remove chicken, cut up and return to broth. Add corn and noodles, simmer until noodles are cooked. Stir in egg. Garnish with parsley.

APPLE BUTTER

½ bushel Mac Intosh apples
4½ quarts cider
4½ pounds sugar
3 tablespoons cinnamon, cloves and allspice (each)

Slice apples, put in a large kettle, add enough water to cook without sticking. When apples are soft put thru a food mill. Meanwhile bring cider to a boil. Add sugar, cooked apple pulp and spices. Transfer to a large roasting pan. Bake at 350° until thick and brown. This should take 6 to 10 hours depending on the depth of pan and moisture in apple pulp. Turn temperature down if sticking occurs. Stir several times during baking. When thick enough ladle into hot jars and seal.

APEAS CAKE

3 cups flour
1 cup sugar
¾ teaspoon salt
2 teaspoon baking powder
½ cup shortening
1 teaspoon baking soda
¾ cup sour milk
1 tablespoon vinegar

Combine flour, sugar, salt, and baking powder. Cut in shortening. Stir baking soda and vinegar into milk, then stir into dry mixture. This is a rather stiff dough. Divide into two 7-inch greased pans. Sprinkle with cinnamon and sugar if desired. Bake at 350° for 45 minutes.

SHOO FLY PIE

2 9-inch pie crusts (unbaked)
3 cups flour
¼ teaspoon salt
1 cup brown sugar
½ cup shortening
1 cup boiling water
1 teaspoon baking soda
1 cup molasses (King syrup or Turkey syrup)

Combine flour, salt and sugar. Cut in shortening to make crumbs. Set aside. Stir boiling water and baking soda into molasses until well combined. Divide liquid mixture between the two pie crusts, top with the crumbs. Bake at 375° for 40 to 45 minutes.

FUNNY CAKE

1 9-inch pie crust (unbaked)
¾ cup sugar
¼ cup shortening
1 egg
¼ cup milk
1 cup flour
1 teaspoon baking powder
½ teaspoon vanilla
½ cup sugar
¼ cup cocoa
½ cup water
½ teaspoon vanilla

Cream ¾ cup sugar and shortening, add egg and beat well. Combine flour and baking powder, add alternately with milk to creamed mixture until well blended. Add vanilla.

Combine ½ cup sugar, cocoa and water in a saucepan, bring to a boil, stirring to make a smooth sauce. Add vanilla. Cool to lukewarm.

Pour sauce into pie crust, spoon cake batter on top. Bake at 375° for 45 minutes.

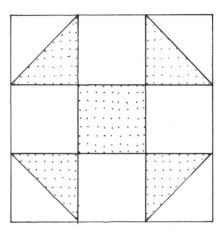

SHOO FLY
Pattern on page 149

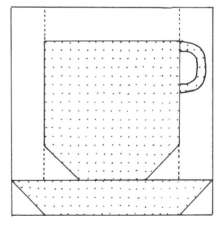

COFFEE CUP
No pattern given

PERKIOMEN HERITAGE

90″ x 90″; made by Variable Star Quilters, quilted by Bertha Rush, 1986.

In combining elements of a local quilt pattern, Perkiomen Valley, and Pennsylvania German folk-art designs, the Variable Star Quilters produced this remarkable quilt which incorporates both patchwork and applique. Fabric, color, and quilting designs all work together in exemplifying the talents of this quilting group.

Plate I

SCHOOLHOUSE

53″ x 82½″; made by Melissa Horn, 1984.

▶ This interesting, well-designed piece is more than just a Schoolhouse quilt. The Schoolhouse blocks were pieced by Variable Star quilting friends and their names are found on the border, making it a special friendship quilt. Unique and original quilting designs of hearts entwined with a chain and hearts-in-hand symbolize the kinship among quilters.

Plate II

FRIENDSHIP STAR

31″ x 31″; made by Nancy Roan, 1987.

▼ A friendship quilt in the traditional sense, but in a wall hanging size, designed specifically to accommodate the names of the Variable Star Quilters. Truly a labor of love.

Plate III

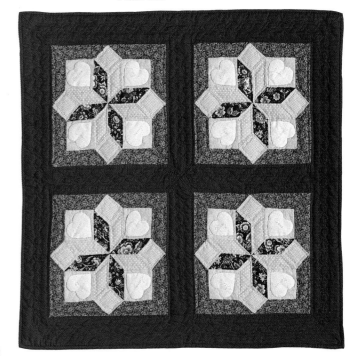

CANADA GOOSE TRACKS

95½″ x 95½″; made by Melissa Horn, 1987.

This unquilted top is made of many colorful scraps, some of which are antique, found in the maker's collection. It was the intent of the maker to produce a quilt that would evoke an image of "a quilt", the kind one would want to snuggle under on a blustery winter night, the quilt one always envisions in their mind as typical. The Canada Goose Tracks pattern and judicious selection of remnants give this quilt an antique quality that fits this image.

Plate IV

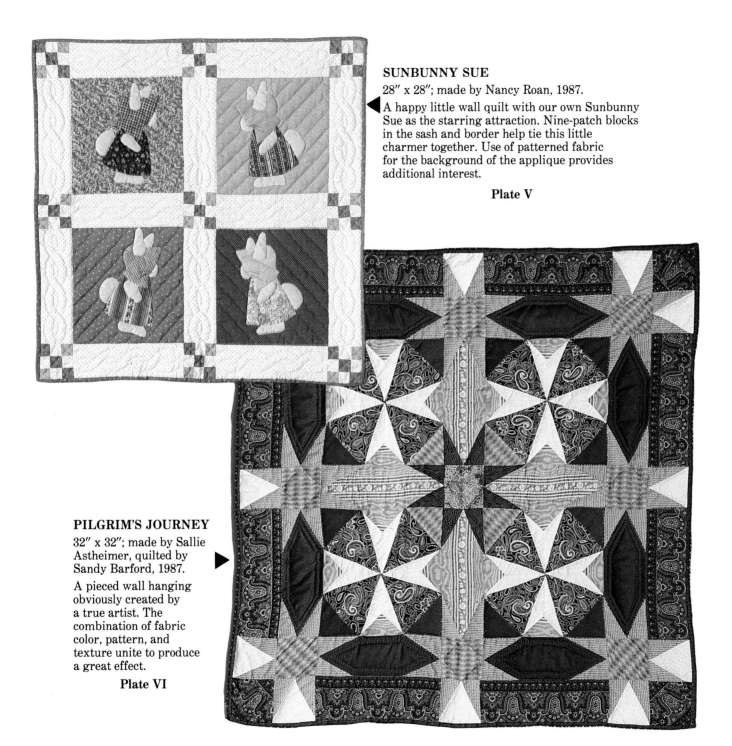

SUNBUNNY SUE

28″ x 28″; made by Nancy Roan, 1987.

A happy little wall quilt with our own Sunbunny Sue as the starring attraction. Nine-patch blocks in the sash and border help tie this little charmer together. Use of patterned fabric for the background of the applique provides additional interest.

Plate V

PILGRIM'S JOURNEY

32″ x 32″; made by Sallie Astheimer, quilted by Sandy Barford, 1987.

A pieced wall hanging obviously created by a true artist. The combination of fabric color, pattern, and texture unite to produce a great effect.

Plate VI

SPIDER WEB

80″ x 94″; made by Sallie Astheimer, quilted by Katie Mae Oelschlager, 1986.

Unusually colorful, bold, and exciting, this pieced country scrap quilt was designed for a boy's room. Quilting on the borders, created and drawn by the quilt maker, is particularly appealing. Included are animals and things of interest to a boy named Tim, a special friend of the "Quiltie Ladies".

Plate VII

PENNSYLVANIA TULIP

85″ x 106″; made by Nancy Roan, 1969.

Striking colors combined with the folk-art quality of this original design give the quilt a very Pennsylvania German look. It was made in 1969, before quilting took the country by storm, using remnants from other sewing projects for the appliqued portions. The quilting designs, some of which are original, also reflect a folk-art origin.

Plate VIII

MILADY'S BASKET

68″ x 68″; made by June Garges, quilted by Sadie Krauss Kriebel, 1985.

The striking combination of pink and black prints with bold sashing make this quilt unusually exciting in color and design. Note the novel manner by which the maker chose to contain her design without using a traditional border. While basket quilts are common, few present the graphic quality so well demonstrated in this example.

Plate IX

PATCHPUSS

85″ x 96″; made by Nancy Roan, 1987.

The felines on this charming quilt appear to be appliqued but are instead pieced with gentle curves. The quilt maker carried the cat theme even further by setting the Patchpuss with Kitty-in-the-Corner blocks and quilting paw prints in the border.

Plate X

PERKIOMEN HERITAGE©

The Perkiomen Heritage quilt contains elements of a fascinating local quilt design, Perkiomen Valley, named for the Perkiomen Creek which flows through Montgomery County in southeastern Pennsylvania. It was designed by the Variable Star quilters as the raffle quilt for the 18th Annual Quilt Show of the National Quilting Association. The center portion is a miniature Perkiomen Valley quilt surrounded by various folk-art motifs of Pennsylvania German origin.

Found in the very center of the quilt is the Virgin Sophia, guardian angel of heavenly wisdom. The unicorn, also found on numerous forms of folk-art, appears in one of the appliqued areas. There are three others on the quilt all taken from fraktur, needlework, tombstone art and dower chests. Pomegranates and currants "grow" from the baskets in the corner blocks. Patterns for some of these motifs are given and could be repeated or you might draw your own by consulting the color photograph. A patchwork variable star of minute dimensions, logo of the variable star quilters, appears in Sophia's heart. It could be embroidered or omitted.

See page 153

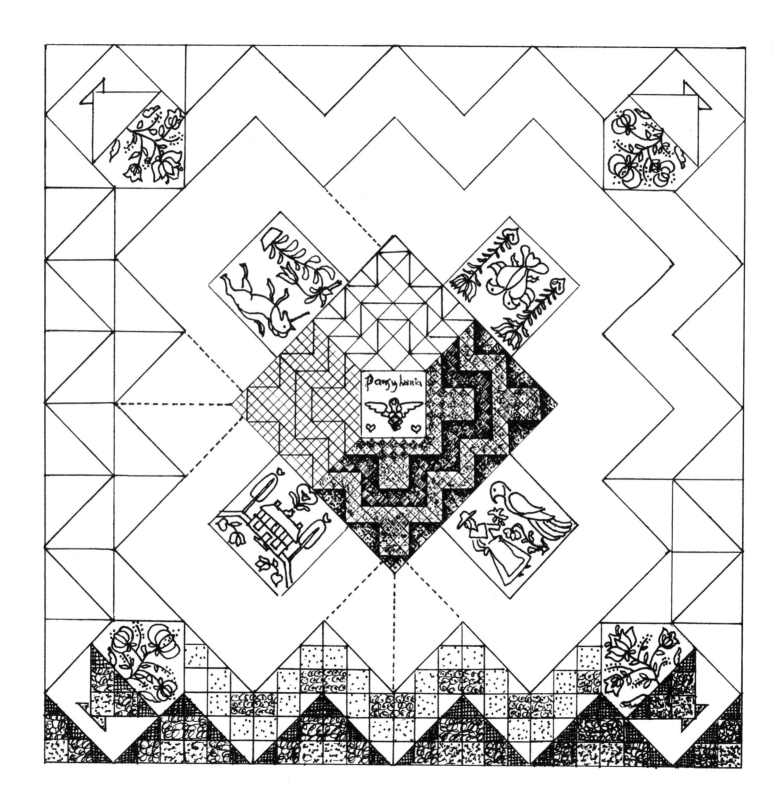

94

To enlarge design: Connect lines to form a grid. Each square equals 1".

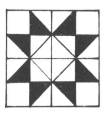

PATTERNS
AND
INSTRUCTIONS
for
Quilt Blocks

General Directions

1. **IMPORTANT**—add seam allowance to all templates.

2. Make a sample block from your templates before cutting out the entire project.

3. Consult a recognized quilting, patchwork or applique manual if you need it. There are many good ones available. Your quilt shop should be able to suggest one to suit your requirements.

4. Templates are included for most but not all patterns.

5. Color and fabric selection are of course a personal thing, but given the nature of this book and the sharing of recipes, we want to include what we are calling color recipes for some blocks. Please feel free to use your own color choice, but if you need inspiration, read over our suggestions—they might help. As many culinary recipes indicate—season to taste—add a dash of your favorite color.

6. Remove selvage before cutting patches—*never* leave selvage in a patch.

7. Shading of the drawings in this book do not always indicate the color or tone suggested in the color recipe for use in that particular block.

8. Be sure to cut patches on the proper grain line.

9. Broken lines on templates indicate that template is to be placed on fold.

   Dotted lines on graphics show seams in background areas (Pieced Teddy Bear, Scottie Dog, Perkiomen Heritage, Evergreen Fir Tree).

QUILTING HINTS

�֍ The hypotenuse of a right-angle triangle equals the square root of the sum of the squares of the sides. $A^2 + B^2 = C^2$

✷ Some quilting patterns (projects, endeavors) require a lot of blood, sweat, and tears. Of these three, blood leaves the most indelible mark on a quilt. If blood gets on your quilt try an old trick—use your saliva to remove it immediately. It works!

✷ Keep a small dish of clean water nearby when doing applique. A small dab will help the fabric behave, making it easier to turn under the seam allowance.

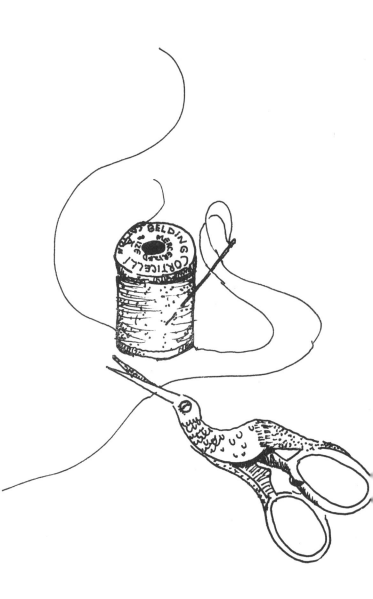

✷ Take care in chosing white and other solid color fabric. Some weaves have a definite grain line which could show up in your finished quilt.

✷ Clip a tiny corner from fabric before washing. This prevents raveling threads.

✷ Take at least three measurements (not including edges) of your quilt and compute an average to determine length of borders.

✷ Templates made from sandpaper stay in place.

✷ Cut background blocks for applique at least 1″ larger than finished size. Trim to size (after applique is completed).

New Year's Day in the Delaware Valley is always a pageant of color as the Mummers strut down Philadelphia Pavements.

Color Recipe: Almost anything goes, but be sure to include gold to represent "dem golden slippers."

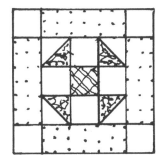

PHILADELPHIA PAVEMENT

Add ¼″ seam allowance to all templates.

Cut:
  A 4 print
  B 1 print
  B 8 background
  C 4 print
  C 4 background

Makes 1—10″ block

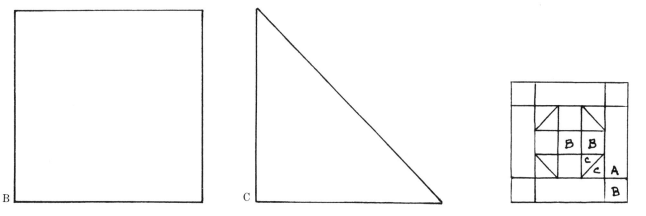

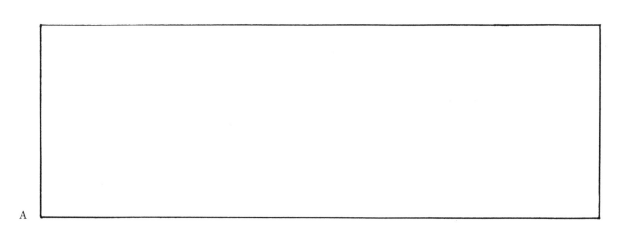

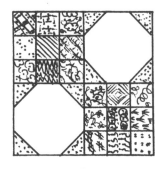

SNOWBALL

Add ¼″ seam allowance
to all templates.

Cut:
  A 18 scrap
  B 8 scrap
  C 2 light

Makes 1—12″ unit as
shown

What would January be without Snowballs? If nature
doesn't comply, make your own.

Color Recipe: Same as Winter Landscape, or this
would be nice in "shades of white."

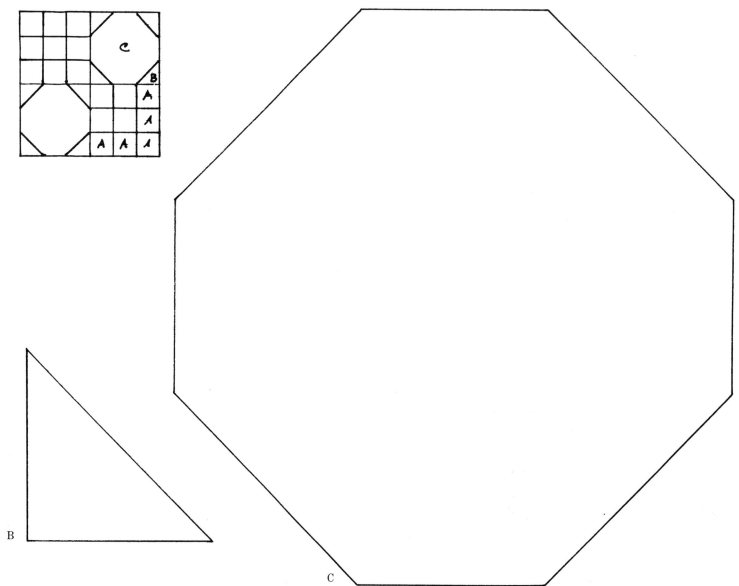

Color your Winter Landscape quilt the way Mother Nature paints her wintry days. Winter hues provide a subdued but nevertheless colorful palette. Look around on snowy days, in the morning, at sunset, when it's cloudy, sunny. . .

Color Recipe: Shades of gray; misty and crisp blues; sunset pink, lavender and orange; forest green.

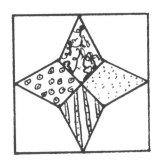

WINTER LANDSCAPE

Add ¼″ seam allowance to all templates.

Cut:
  A 4 white
  B 4 scrap

Makes 1—9″ block

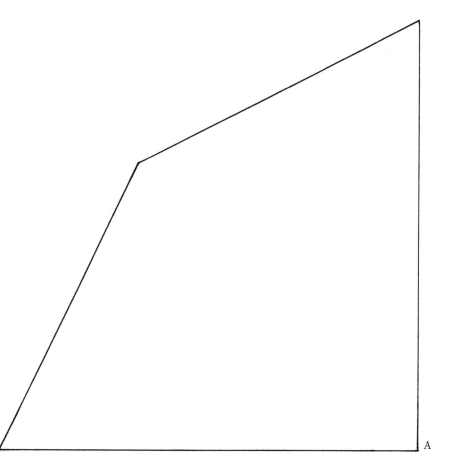

A

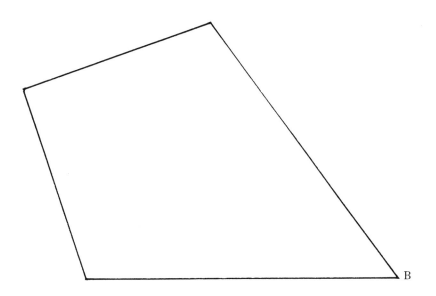

B

101

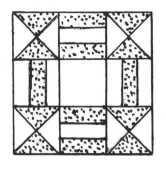

**CUPID'S
ARROW**

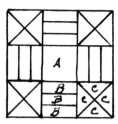

Lucky you to be struck by Cupid's Arrow. Our 19th century example of this block was done in blue and white. Perfect hit!

Color Recipe: We'd like it in red and white.

Add ¼″ seam allowance to all templates.

Cut:
   A 1 light
   B 6 light
   B 6 dark
   C 8 light
   C 8 dark

Makes 1—9″ block

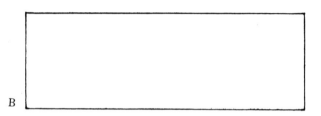

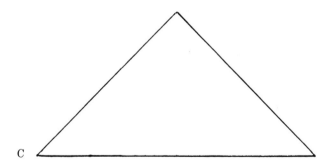

A non-caloric but sweet valentine for someone you love.

Color Recipe: You know your sweetheart's favorite color.

SWEETHEART HONEY BEE©

Add ¼″ seam allowance to all templates.

Cut:
A 1 color 1
A 4 color 2
A 4 color 3
B 4 background
C 4 background
D 8 color 1
E 4 color 2

Makes 1—10½″ block

A

B

C

103

PRESIDENT'S
STAR

Add ¼″ seam allowance
to all templates.

Cut:
   A 4 background
   B 5 red
   B 4 white
   C 20 white
   C 28 blue
   D 4 background

Makes 1—12″ block

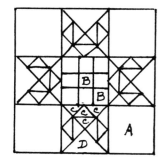

Two of our most famous presidents were born in February. A quilt of President's Star blocks could make you famous too.

Color Recipe: Obviously red, white, blue and gold.

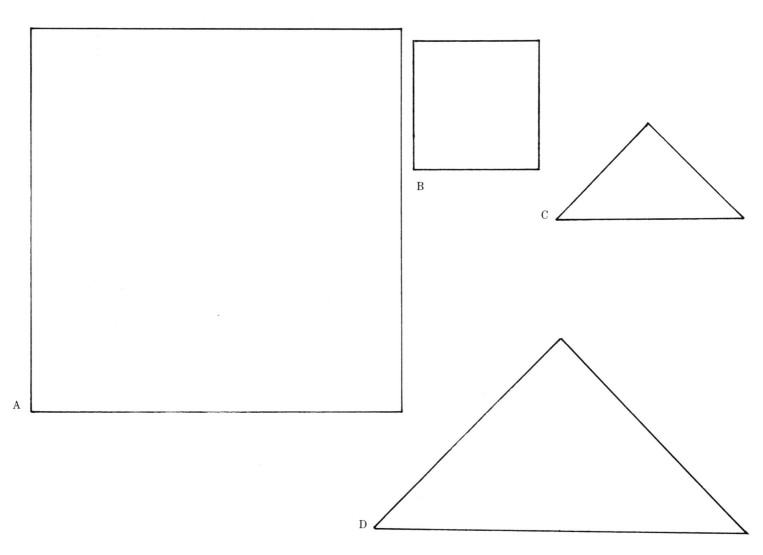

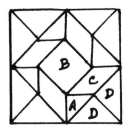

Brisk March winds are Mother Nature's way of sweeping the countryside. Increase the "velocity" by using stripes.

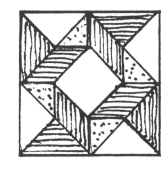

WINDBLOWN SQUARE

Add ¼" seam allowance to all templates.

Cut:
- A 4 print
- B 1 background
- C 4 stripe
- D 4 background
- D 4 stripe

Makes 1—8" block

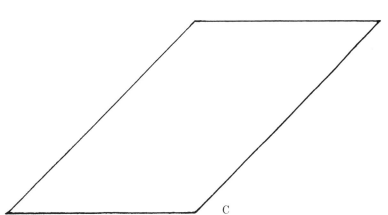

C

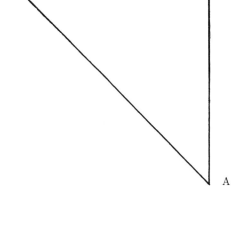

A

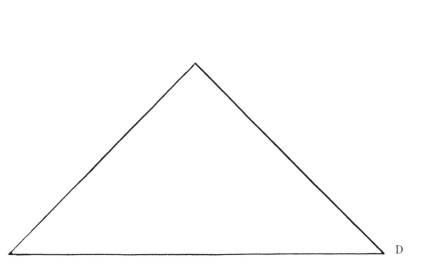

D

B

LUCKY IRISH CHAIN©

Add ¼″ seam allowance to all templates.

BLOCK 1
Cut:
  A 4 white
  A 9 print
  A 12 green

BLOCK 2
Cut:
  A 4 green
  B 4 white
  C 4 green
  D 4 white

Each makes a 10″ block.

Even the non-Irish can't help warming up to an Irish tune, and most quilt admirers find Double Irish Chain to their liking. We've added a four-leaf clover to ours for an additional measure of Irish luck. That's no blarney!

Color Recipe: Green, of course!

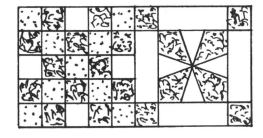

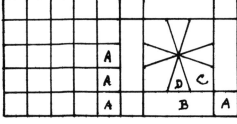

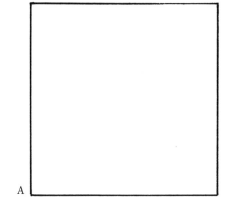

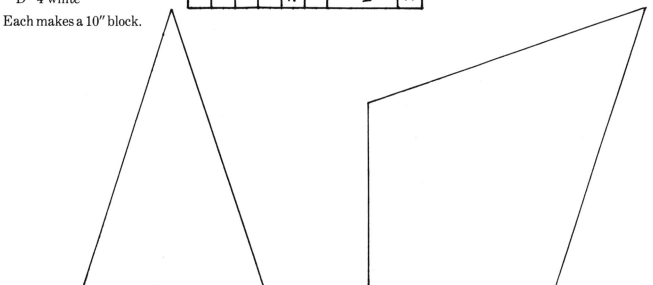

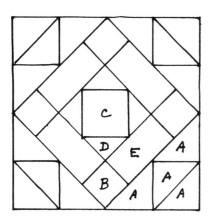

A harbinger of spring. We want this block to represent the early spring wildflower, not a clergyman named Jack.

Color Recipe: Shades of green, brown, purple and off-white.

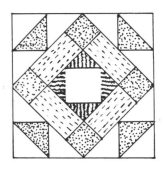

JACK-IN-THE-PULPIT

Add ¼″ seam allowance to all templates.

Cut:
- A 12 background
- A 4 contrast
- B 4 contrast
- C 1 background
- D 4 dark
- E 4 light

Makes 1—16″ block

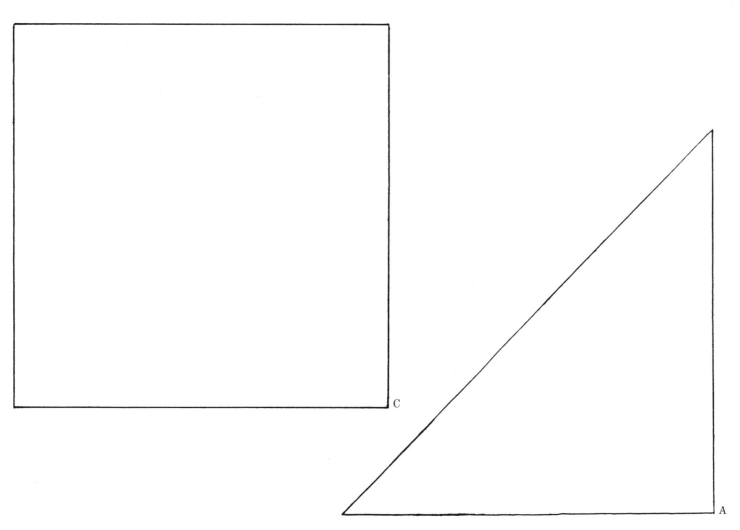

(Continued on page 108)

**JACK-IN-THE-
PULPIT**
(continued)

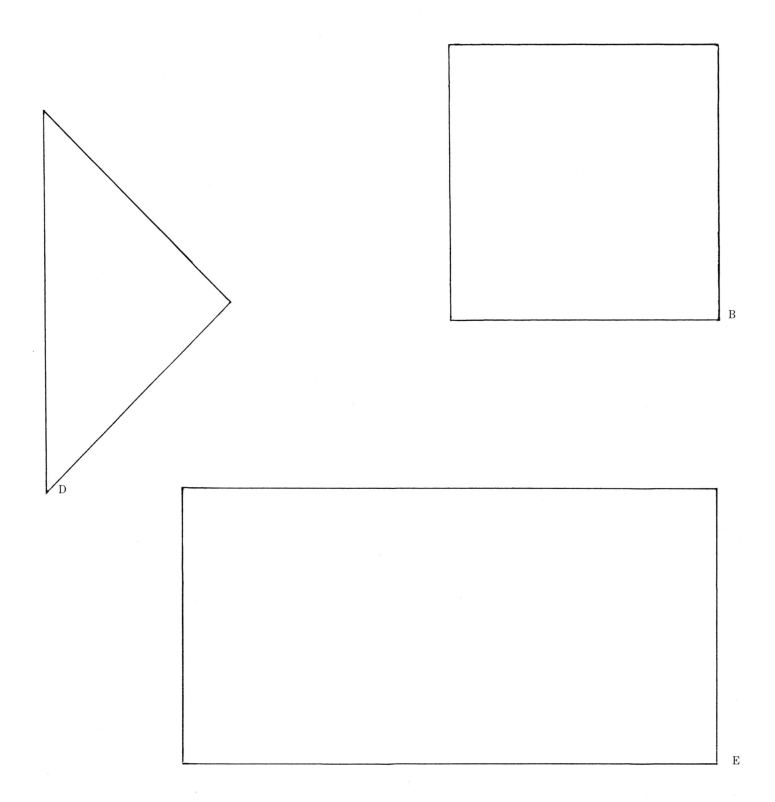

D

B

E

Rid your attic or cellar or your entire house of Spider Webs in a bout of enthusiastic house-cleaning. Or rid your fabric closet of an accumulation of scraps in a quick, enthusiastic piecing of Spider Web.

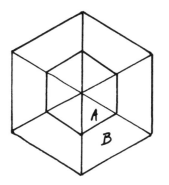

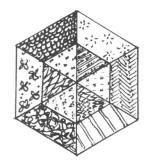

SPIDER WEB

Add ¼″ seam allowance to all templates.

Cut:
- A 3 light
- A 3 dark
- B 3 light
- B 3 dark

Makes 1 hexagon, 6″ on each side.

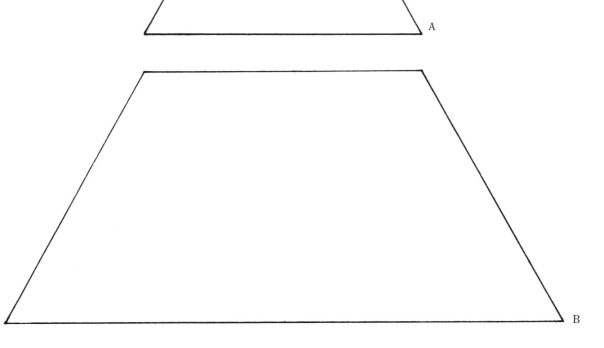

A

B

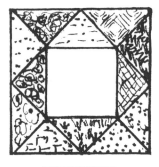

ECONOMY

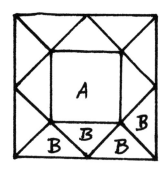

If you escape the Ides of March, watch out for the "Ides of April" or Income Tax Day—a very appropriate time for the Economy block.

Color Recipe: Scrape the bottom of your scrap bag, and color it prudently.

Add ¼" seam allowance to all templates.

Cut:
  A 1 background
  B 12 scrap

Makes 1—8" block

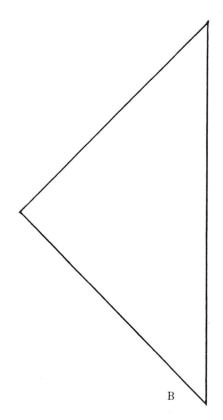

An adaptation of a well-known quilt personality, this block is perfect for the Easter season.

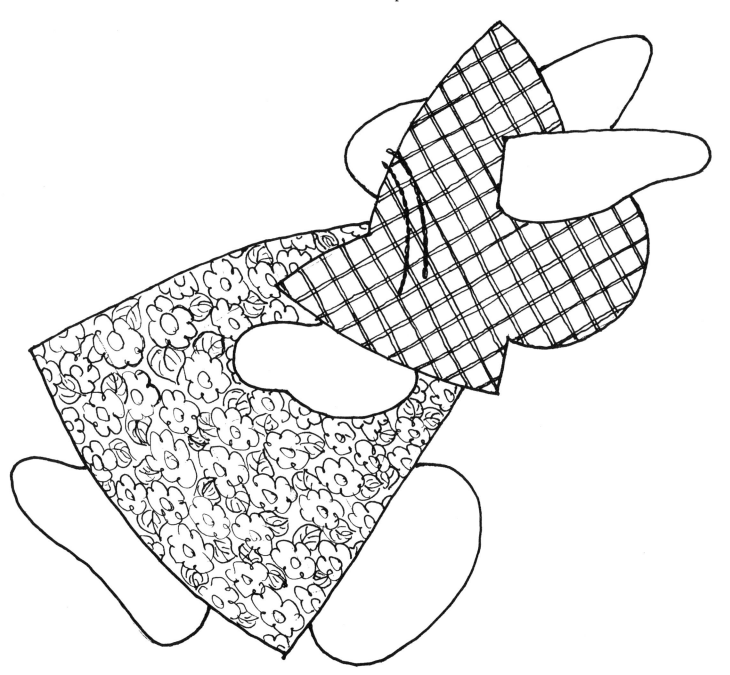

SUNBUNNY SUE©

Cut templates from actual size drawing. Add ¼" seam allowance to all templates. Add details with embroidery. Cut background square to finish a minimum 9½" square.

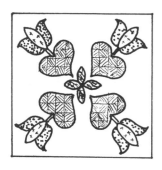

PENNSYLVANIA TULIP©

An original applique with a true Pennsylvania Dutch flavor.

Color Recipe: Give it a folk art look by using traditional primary colors.

Add ¼″ seam allowance to all templates.

Cut:
   4 hearts
   4 tulip centers
   4 tulip petals
   4 tulip petals (reverse)
   4 leaves
   Bias strip to finish ⅜″ wide for stems
   1 background square to finish 18″

Makes 1—18″ block

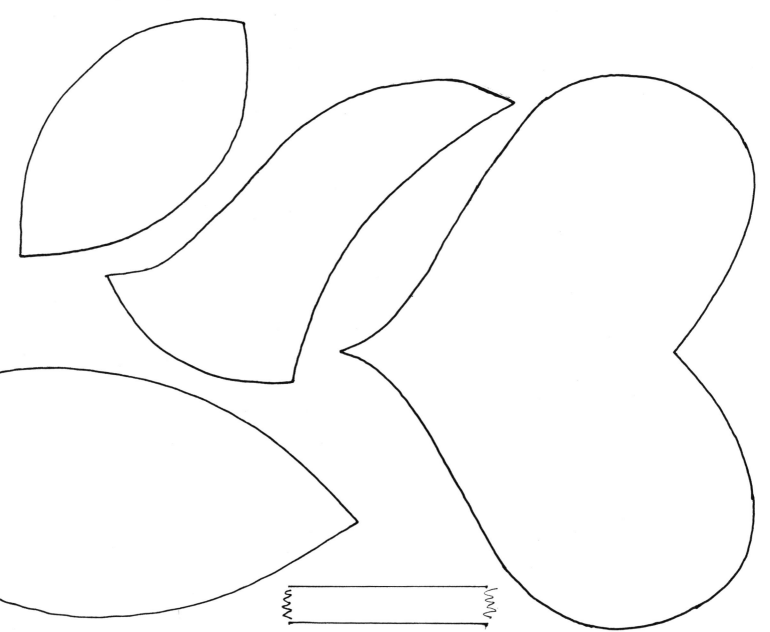

A traditional basket, with an innovative handle. This pattern was drafted from a stiking example in pink and black sewn by one of our members.

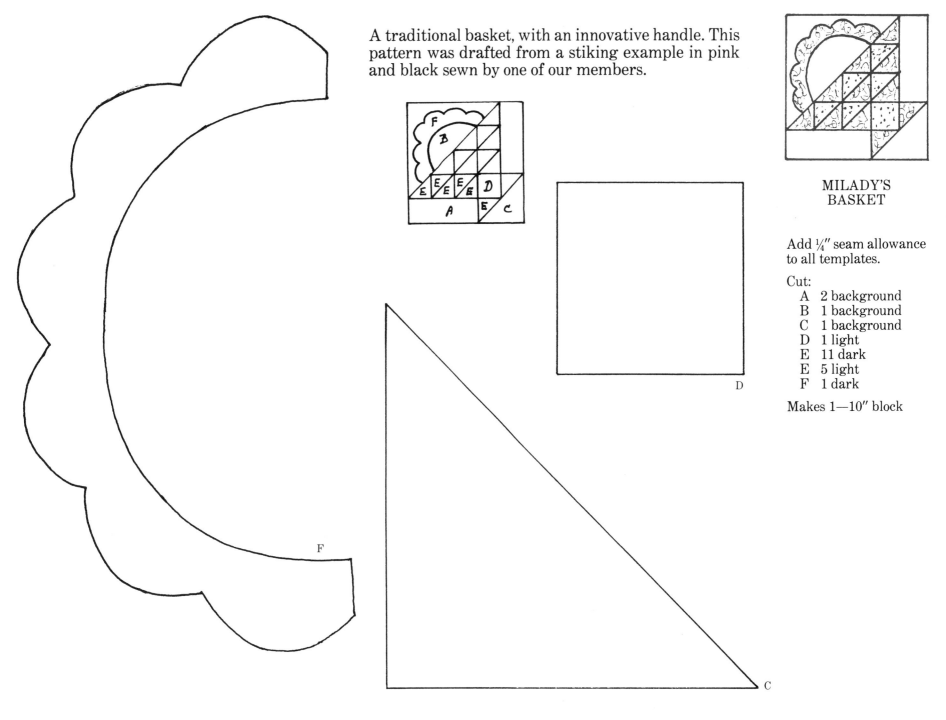

MILADY'S BASKET

Add ¼″ seam allowance to all templates.

Cut:
- A 2 background
- B 1 background
- C 1 background
- D 1 light
- E 11 dark
- E 5 light
- F 1 dark

Makes 1—10″ block

(Continued on page 114)

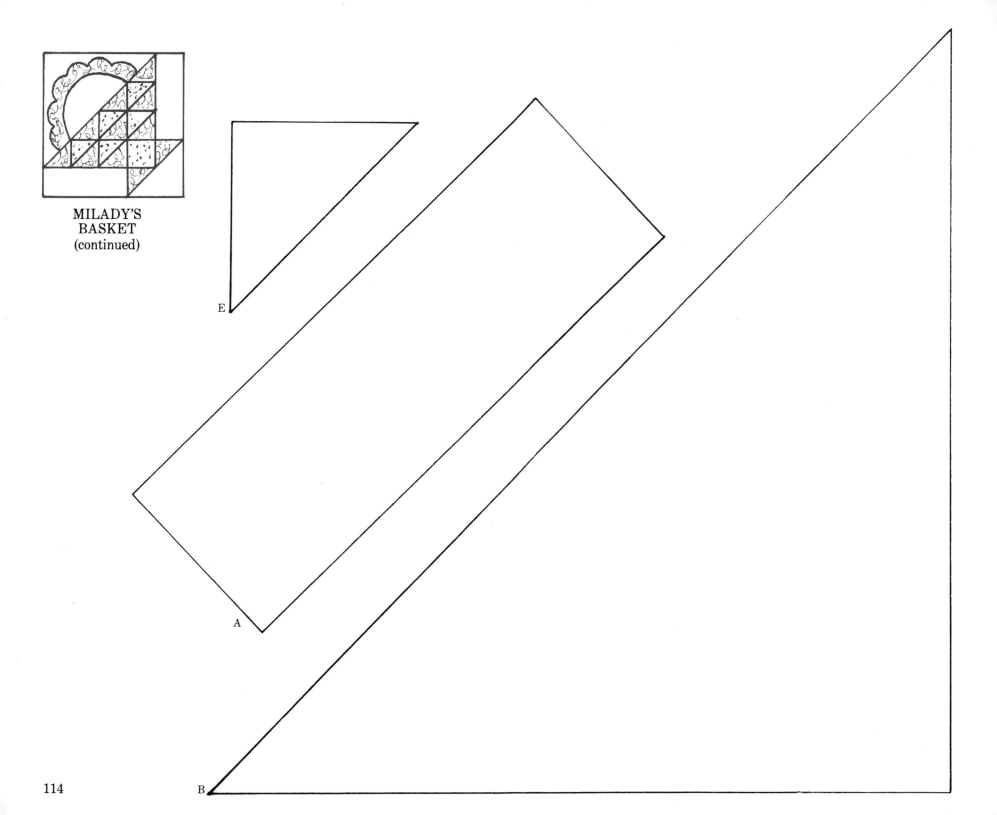

MILADY'S
BASKET
(continued)

E

A

B

Bird lovers as well as quilters should find this block interesting. Pay homage to your local songbird population by exercising your "nesting instincts"—make a quilt of this block.

Color Recipe: Consult a bird guide in selecting fabric and use plumage colors. Also consider subtle bird egg hues, along with leafy greens.

BIRD'S
NEST

Add ¼″ seam allowance to all templates.

Cut:
    A   4 color 1
    B   4 color 1
    B   12 background
    C   20 background
    D   8 background
    E   9 color 2

Makes 1—10″ block

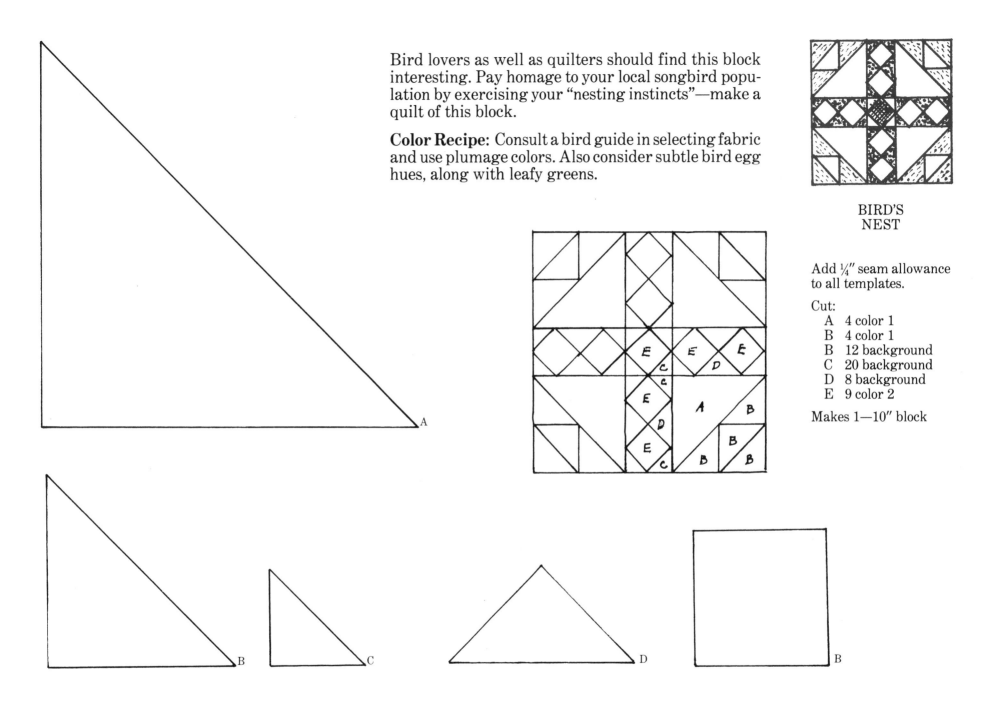

115

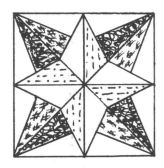

MOTHER'S DELIGHT

Add ¼″ seam allowance to all templates.

Cut:

   A 4 color 1
   A 4 color 2 (reverse)
   B 4 color 3
   B 4 color 4 (reverse)
   C 8 background

Makes 1—12″ block

Probably one of your Mother's Delights is that you are a quilter.

Color Recipe: Do this in your mother's favorite colors.

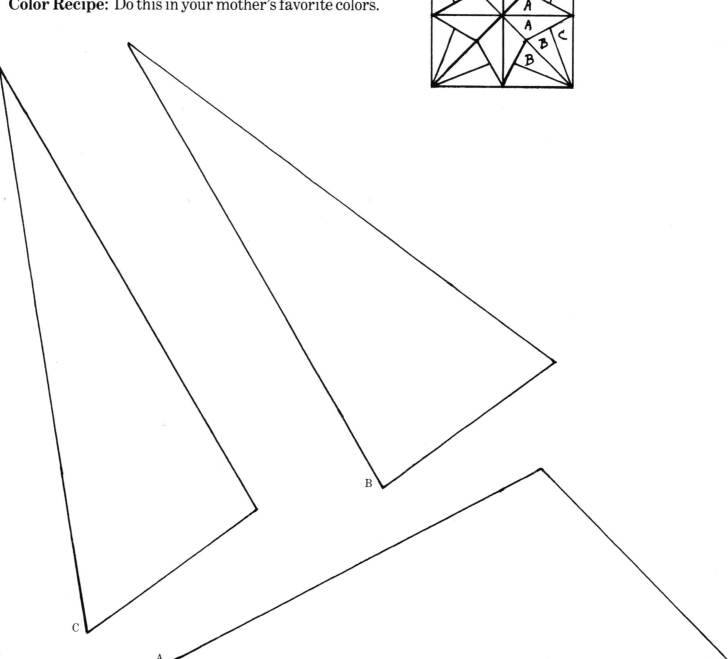

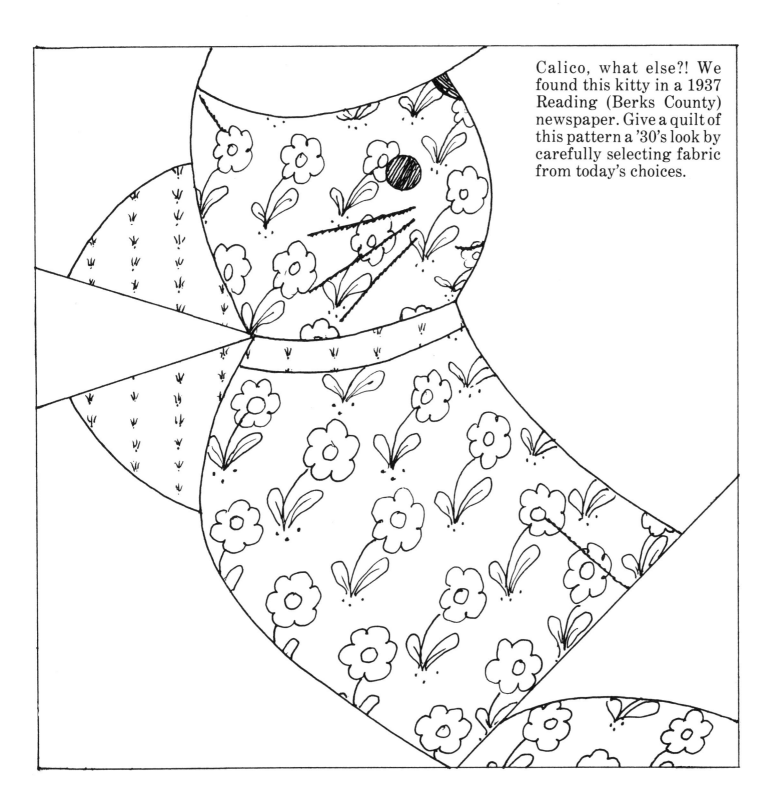

Calico, what else?! We found this kitty in a 1937 Reading (Berks County) newspaper. Give a quilt of this pattern a '30's look by carefully selecting fabric from today's choices.

PATCHPUSS

This is a pieced block. Cut templates from actual size drawing. Add ¼″ seam allowance to all templates. Add details with embroidery. Makes 1—8″ block.

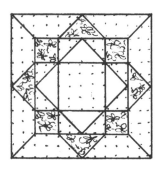

**BRIDE'S
CHOICE**

Add ¼″ seam allowance
to all templates.

Cut:
A   8 medium color 1
B   1 light
C   8 medium color 2
D   4 dark
E   4 dark
E   4 medium color 3

Makes 1—12″ block

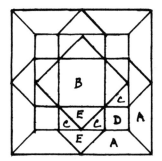

June is the month of brides; what more suitable choice
for a bride than a quilt of this pattern.

Color Recipe: Capture the brilliance of the colors
reflected from the facets and the depths of a perfect
diamond and make a perfect quilt.

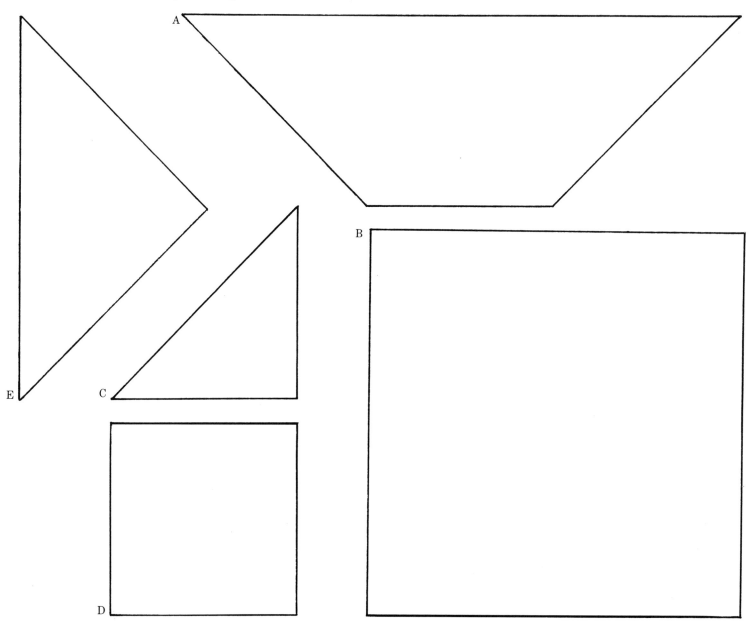

An original by one of us; try this interlocking block for an unusual kitchen wall-hanging.

Color Recipe: We suggest coral and cream, reminiscent of our Crab Bisque; or use blue fabric for a blue crab version.

CRAB©

Add ¼″ seam allowance to all templates.

For 1—9″ crab, cut:
- A   1
- B   4
- C   4

Makes 1—9″ crab

This pattern is constructed of squares, as indicated by the bold lines on the piecing diagram. Consideration of the color of the adjoining square is of utmost importance because of the interlocking nature of the design. Diagram shows two complete squares plus border treatment (templates for border—B, C, D, and E).

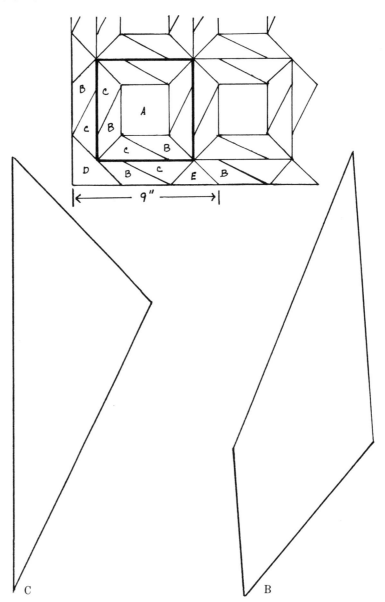

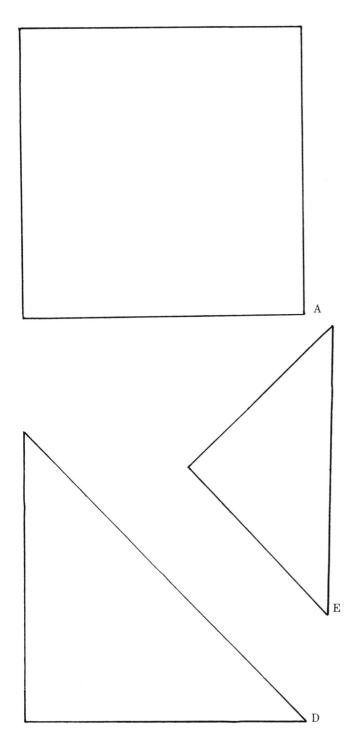

119

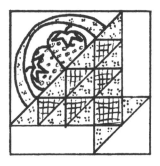

**STRAWBERRY
BASKET©**

This is a pieced block.
Only the handle and
calyx are appliqued.
Embroider stems. Add
¼″ seam allowance to all
templates.

Cut:
  A 2 background
  B 2 background
  C 1 light
  D 1 background
  E 11 dark
  E 5 light
  F 2 red (strawberry)
  G 2 green (calyx)
  H 1 dark (handle)

Makes 1—10″ block

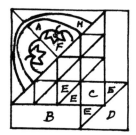

Who can resist the bright red juicy strawberries so
plentiful in June? We couldn't, so here they are,
nestled in a traditional basket. You will note the
berries evolved from Hearts and Gizzards pattern—
quite a transformation, wouldn't you say?

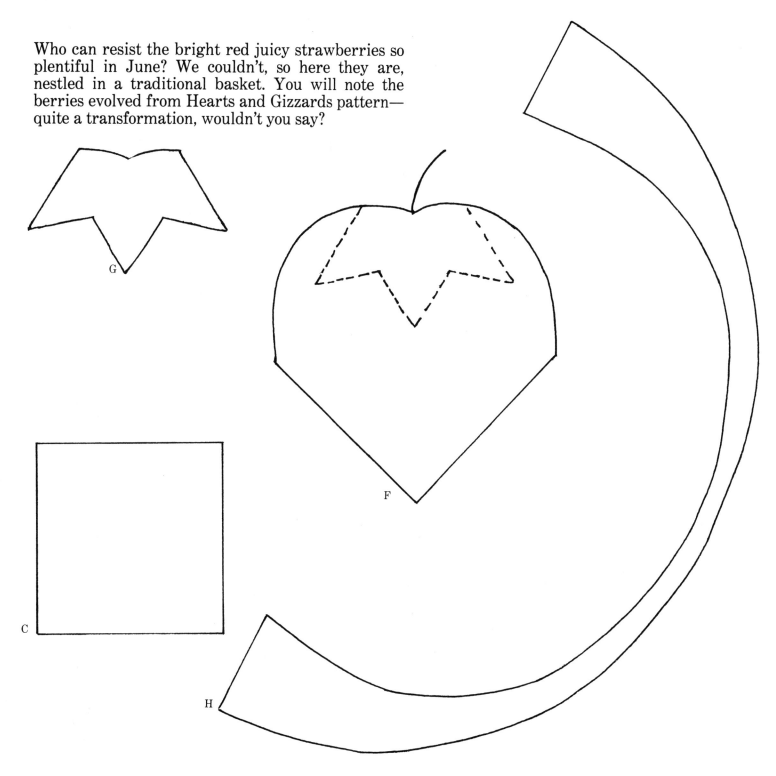

(Continued on page 121)

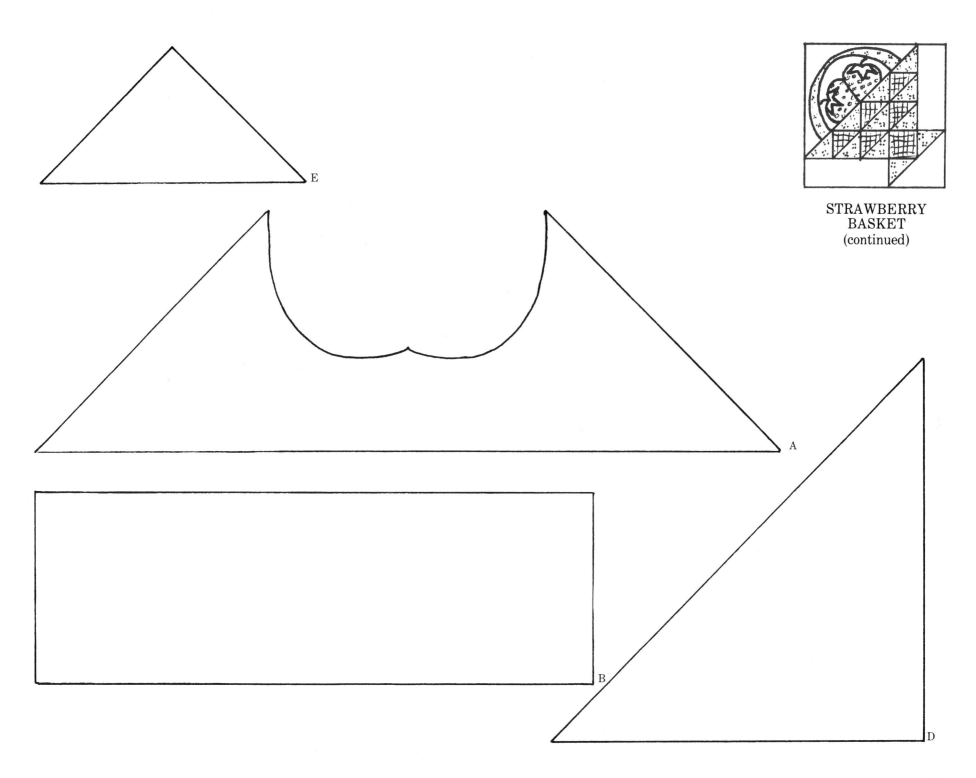

STRAWBERRY
BASKET
(continued)

E

A

B

D

121

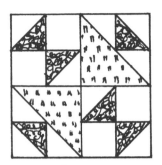

OLD MAID'S
PUZZLE

Add ¼″ seam allowance
to all templates.

Cut:
   A 2 medium
   B 6 dark
   B 10 background
   C 4 background

Makes 1—12″ block

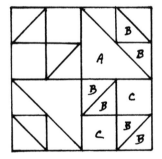

Was our maid too engrossed in solving the puzzle?
Perhaps "Steps to the Altar" would have been a wiser
choice.

Color Recipe: Lavender and old lace, cameo tan and
dusty blue.

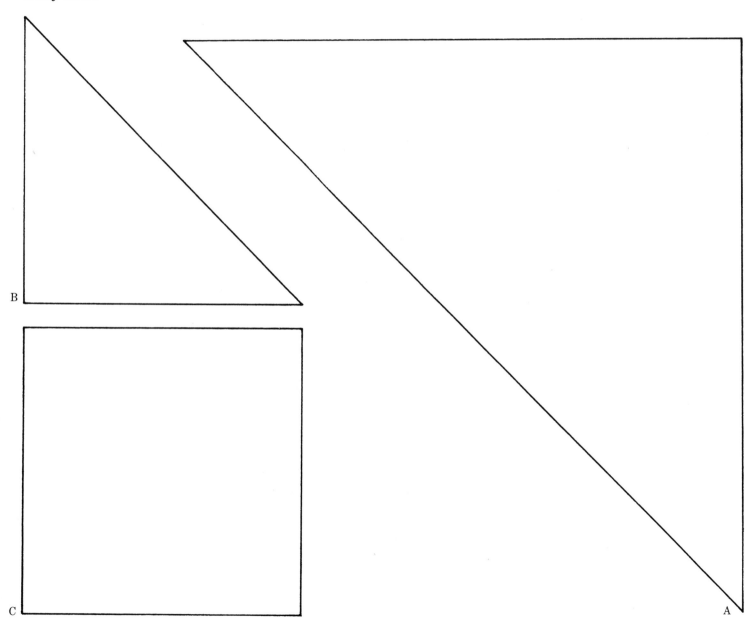

122

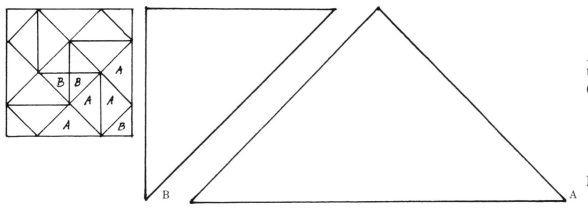

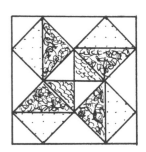

JULY
FOURTH
Add ¼″ seam allowance
to all templates.

Cut:
   A   4 background
   A   4 medium
   B   4 background
   B   2 medium
   B   2 light
Makes 1— 8″ block

A block designed to recognize John Philip Sousa for his contribution to our enjoyment of a traditional band concert.

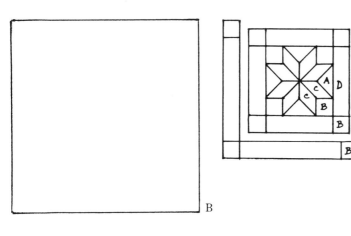

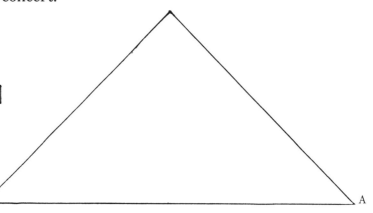

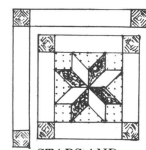

STARS AND
STRIPES FOREVER
Add ¼″ seam allowance
to all templates.

Cut:
   A   4 background
   B   4 background
   B   4 dark
   C   4 light
   C   4 dark (reverse)
   D   4 light

Makes 1—12″ block, not
including joining sash.

For each 2″ wide join-
ing sash cut:
   1—12″ x 2″ light
   1 of template B dark

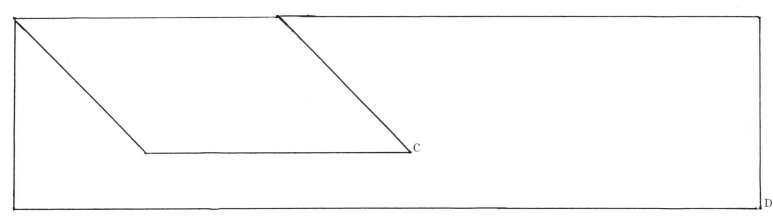

123

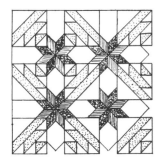

POSEIDON'S STAR©

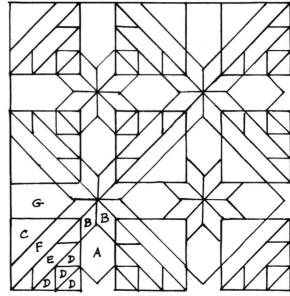

The ubiquitous quilter's star and the sailboat pattern combine in this nautical design inspired by the Greek god of the sea. If you've got your sailboat hitched to a star, take off and let the challenge of this not-too-easy design provide you with a bit of high adventure.

Color Recipe: Deep, deep blue, moonlit ivory, starry shades of gold, moonlit blue.

Add ¼″ seam allowance to all templates. Graphic shows one unit. Make three more and give each a quarter turn when setting to make a balanced design. Note three-dimensional star (upper left in graphic) will appear in each corner.

Cut:
    A   8 background
    B   16 color 1
    B   16 color 2
    C   9 background
    D   45 background
    D   9 boat color
    E   9 boat color
    F   9 boat color
    G   4 background

Makes 1—24″ unit.

(Continued on page 125)

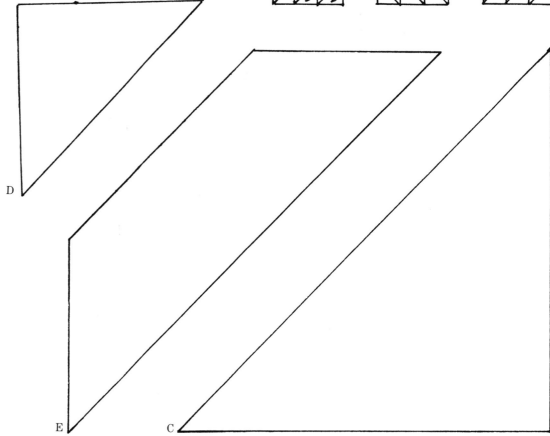

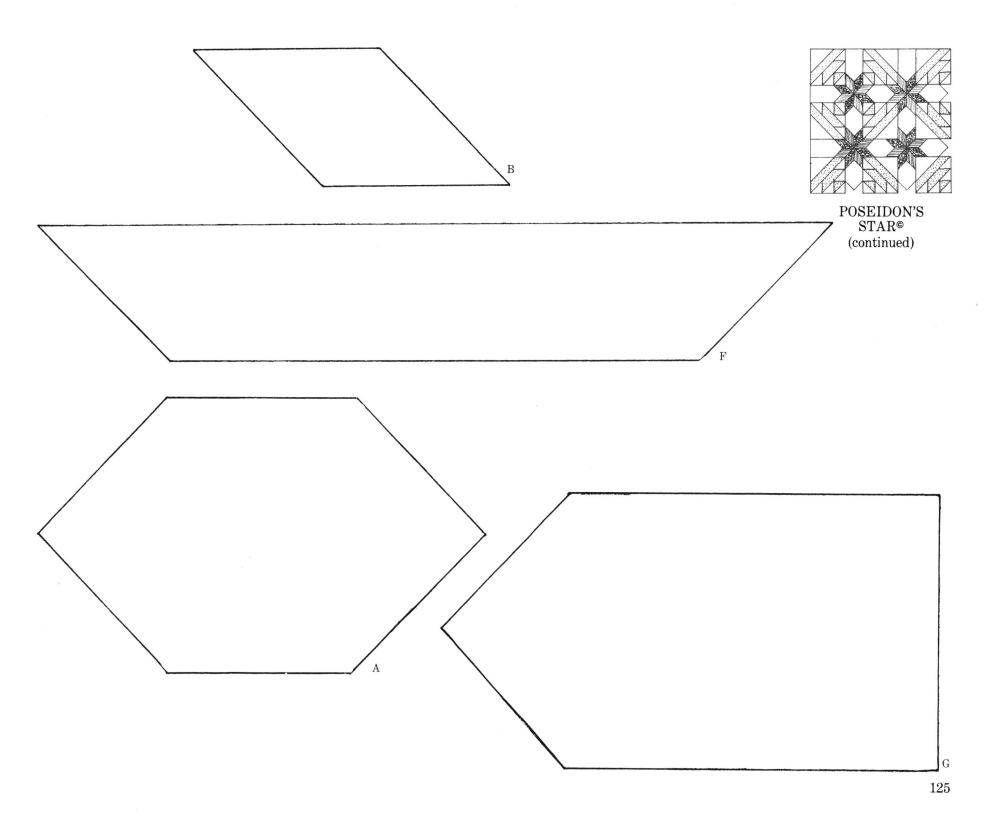

B

POSEIDON'S
STAR©
(continued)

F

A

G

125

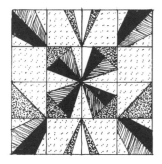

FIREWORKS©

Remember the last fireworks you saw? The colors should still be embedded in your mind's eye—even if your ears have stopped ringing. This original design captures the burst of color and light, but not the sound.

Color Recipe: Fireworks colors of red-orange, lightning yellow, electric blue.

Add ¼″ seam allowance to all templates.

Cut:
- A 2
- B 4
- C 4
- C 4 (reverse)
- D 4
- D 4 (reverse)
- E 2
- E 2 (reverse)
- F 2
- F 2 (reverse)
- G 2
- G 2 (reverse)
- H 4
- I 4
- I 4 (reverse)
- J 4
- J 4 (reverse)

Makes 1—16″ block

(Continued on page 127)

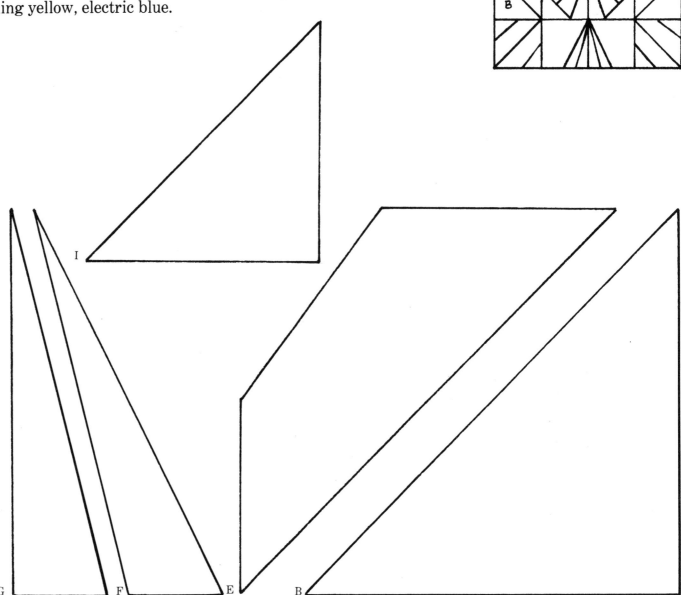

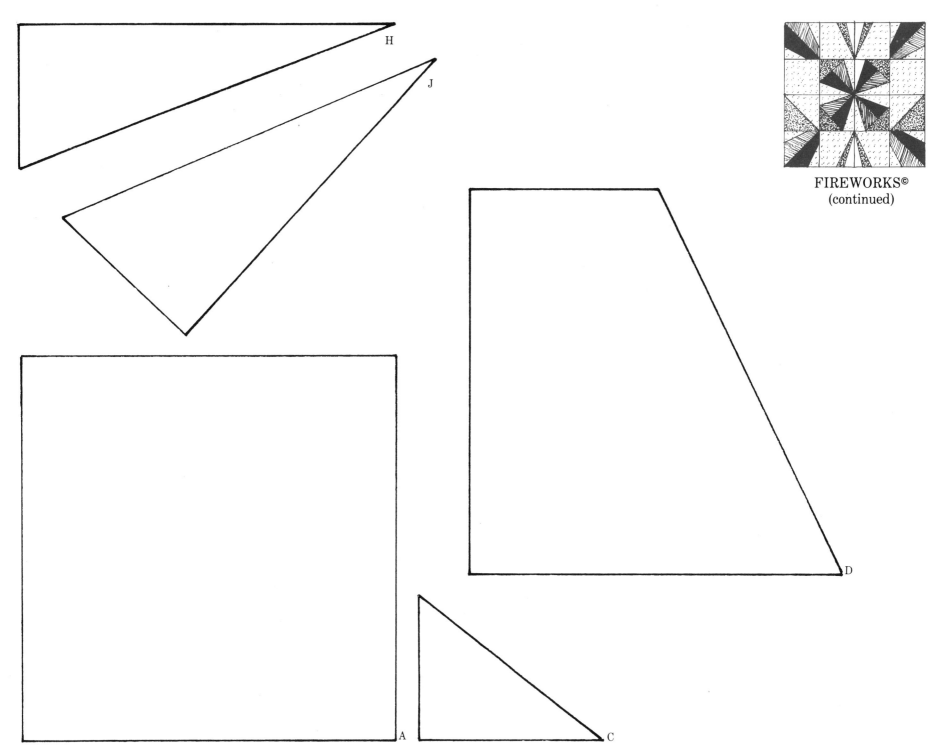

FIREWORKS©
(continued)

127

SAND
CASTLES©

Add ¼″ seam allowance
to all templates.

Cut:
- A 4 sand
- B 30 sand
- B 38 water values
- C 4 contrast
- D 4 brown
- D 4 sand (reverse)
- D 4 background
- D 4 background
   (reverse)
- E 4 contrast

Makes 1—14″ block

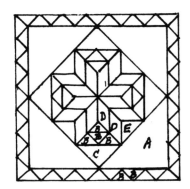

A combination of Castle Keep and Ocean Waves washes up memories of those venerable castles of sand constructed on the beach.

Color Recipe: Sand and surf and colorful beach umbrellas should provide enough and varied color to inspire any quilter.

This complex-looking pattern is very simple to piece, and is most effective in two colors. Care must be taken when setting to make it just right.

Color Recipe: Try it in milk chocolate brown and nougat tan to satisfy your sweet tooth.

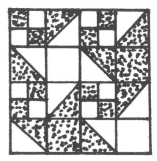

MILKY
WAY

Add ¼″ seam allowance to all templates.

Cut:
   A   8 dark
   A   8 light
   B   2 dark
   B   2 light
   C   8 dark
   C   8 light

Makes 1—8″ block

B

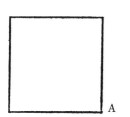

A

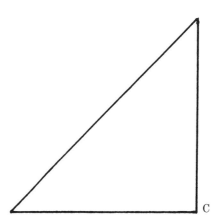

C

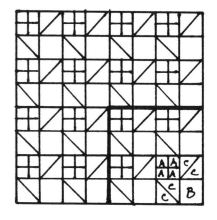

SCOTTIE
DOG©

Add ¼″ seam allowance to all templates. Seams for piecing background are indicated by dotted lines.

Cut:

- A 1 background
- B 1 black
- C 1 background
- C 2 black
- D 4 black
- E 2 background
- E 2 background (reverse)
- F 1 black
- G 2 background
- H 1 background
- I 2 background

Makes 1—12″ x 14″ block

July and August bring the hot, humid Dog Days. Don't wilt—celebrate with a crisp, cool, perky Scottie quilt in black and white, or cool it and use whatever color you'd like. No sweat!

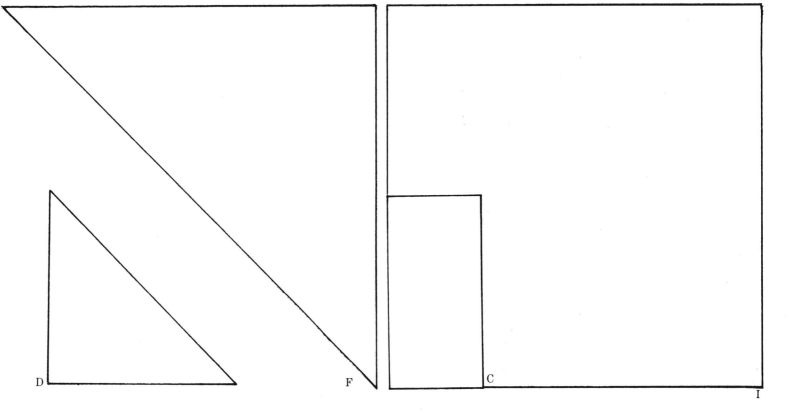

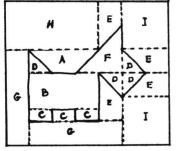

(Continued on page 131)

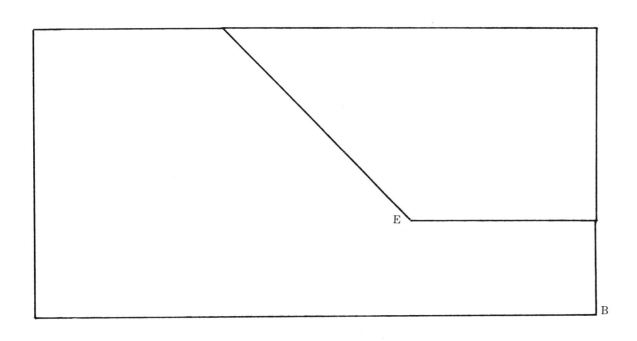

E

B

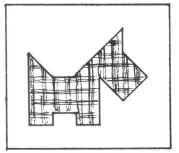

SCOTTIE
DOG©
(continued)

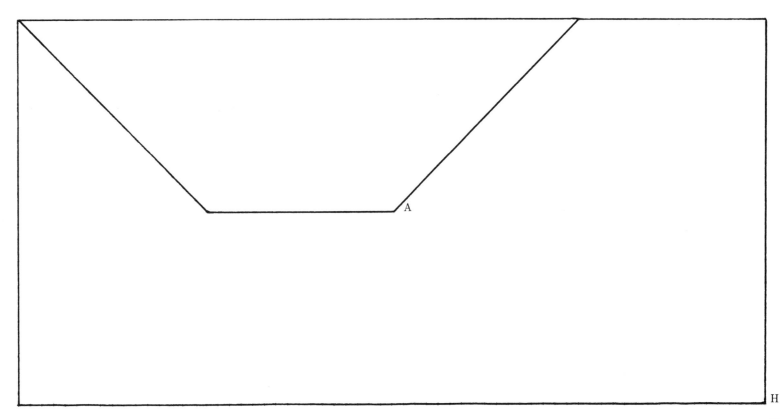

A

H

131

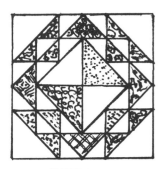

CORN AND BEANS

One of the few traditional blocks referring to food. Call it Succotash, if you will.

Color Recipe: Various pinks, browns, greens, yellows, whites. Dry beans come in a variety of colors and make an interesting combination for this patch.

Add ¼″ seam allowance to all templates.

Cut:
   A 6 background
   A 2 scrap
   B 12 background
   B 20 scrap
   C 4 scrap

Makes 1—12″ block

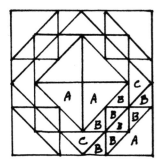

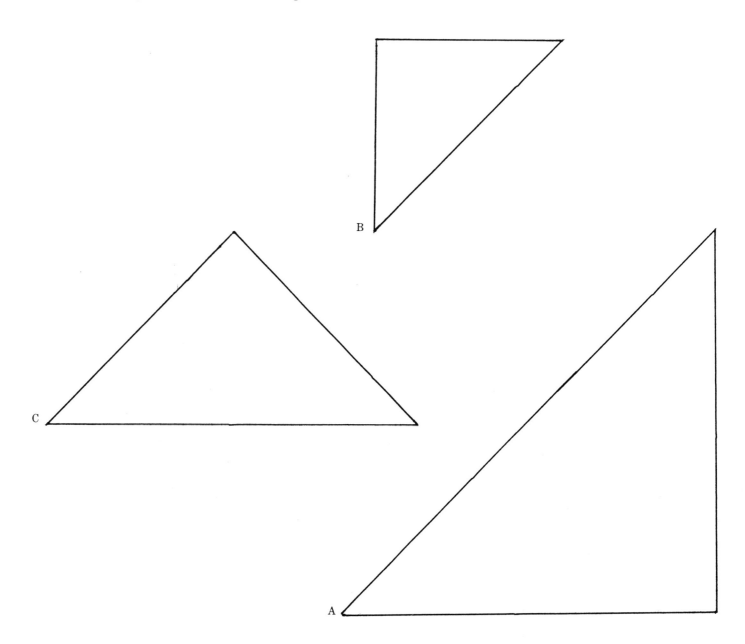

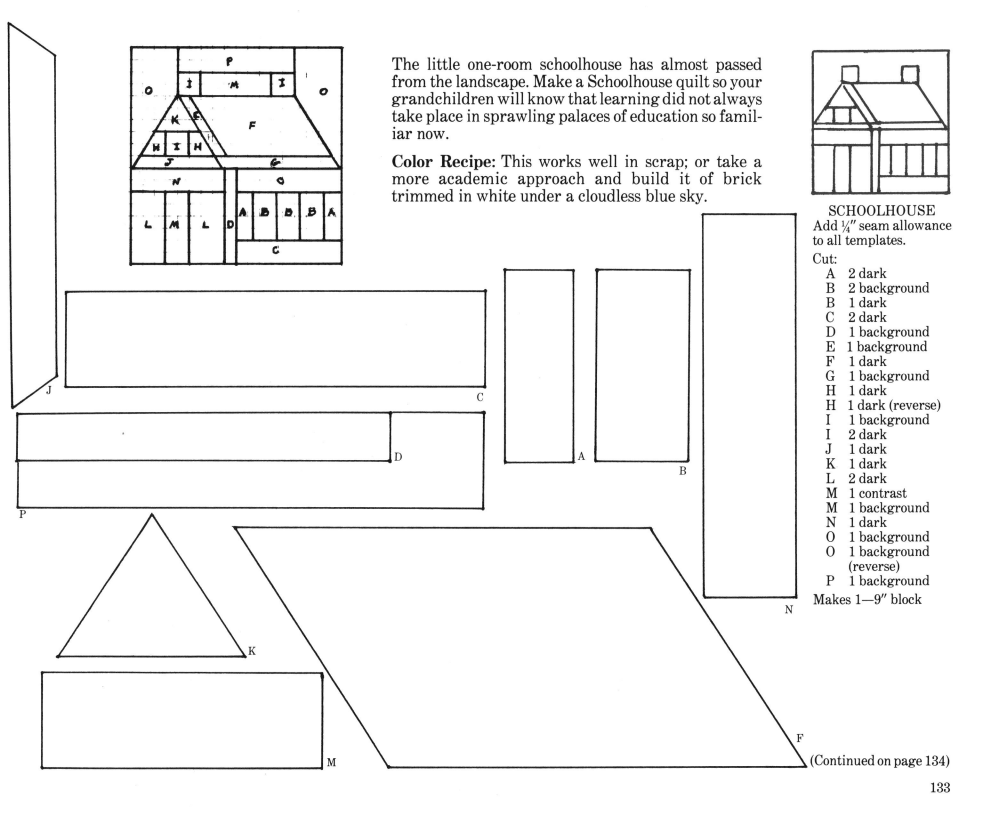

The little one-room schoolhouse has almost passed from the landscape. Make a Schoolhouse quilt so your grandchildren will know that learning did not always take place in sprawling palaces of education so familiar now.

Color Recipe: This works well in scrap; or take a more academic approach and build it of brick trimmed in white under a cloudless blue sky.

SCHOOLHOUSE
Add ¼″ seam allowance to all templates.
Cut:
  A 2 dark
  B 2 background
  B 1 dark
  C 2 dark
  D 1 background
  E 1 background
  F 1 dark
  G 1 background
  H 1 dark
  H 1 dark (reverse)
  I 1 background
  I 2 dark
  J 1 dark
  K 1 dark
  L 2 dark
  M 1 contrast
  M 1 background
  N 1 dark
  O 1 background
  O 1 background (reverse)
  P 1 background
Makes 1—9″ block

(Continued on page 134)

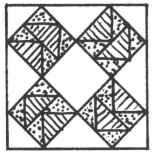

SCHOOLHOUSE
(continued)

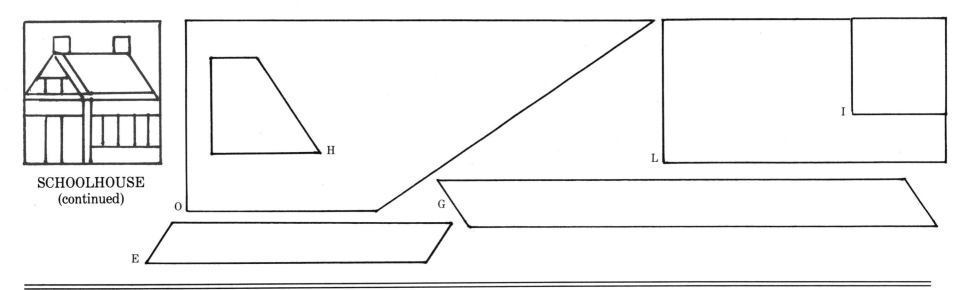

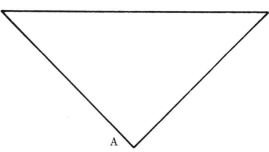

MIGRATING
HAWKS©

Add ¼″ seam allowance
to all templates.

Cut:
- A 8 brown scrap
- A 4 background (sky)
- B 4 background (sky)
- C 16 contrast
- D 1 background (sky)

Makes 1—8″ block

Nearby Hawk Mountain is on the migratory flyway, and many people visit there to observe the migration of hawks and other birds.

Color Recipe: A subtle tan stripe will help give this patch added movement. The color of a September sky provides a natural background.

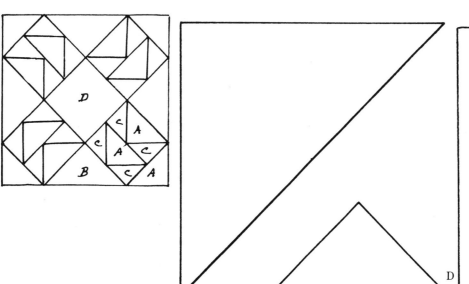

An adaptation of a circa 1930 pattern called Allentown, re-worked to capture the color and exuberance of a county fair.

Color Recipe: Night-sky blue and illuminated white; the midway could also suggest other color ideas.

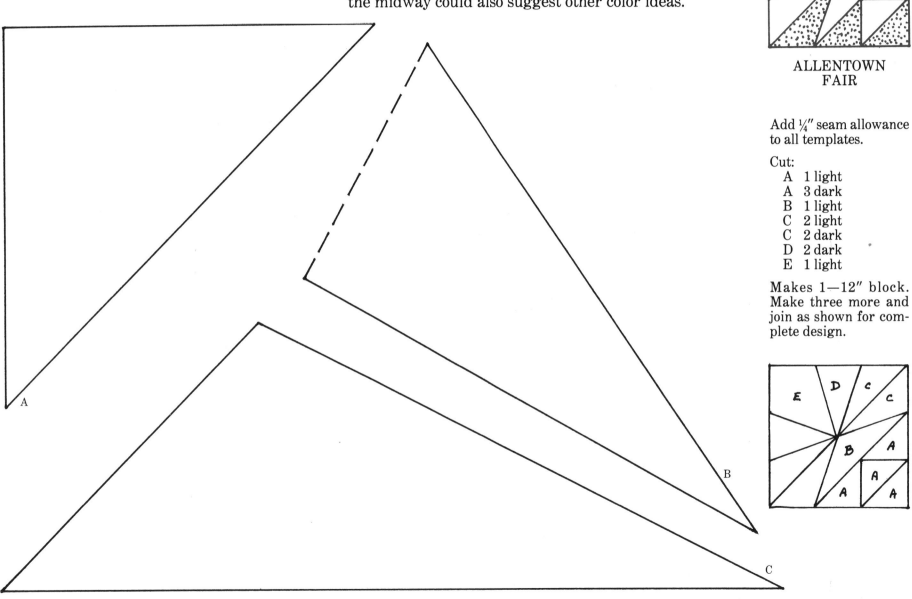

ALLENTOWN
FAIR

Add ¼″ seam allowance to all templates.

Cut:
A   1 light
A   3 dark
B   1 light
C   2 light
C   2 dark
D   2 dark
E   1 light

Makes 1—12″ block. Make three more and join as shown for complete design.

(Continued on page 136)

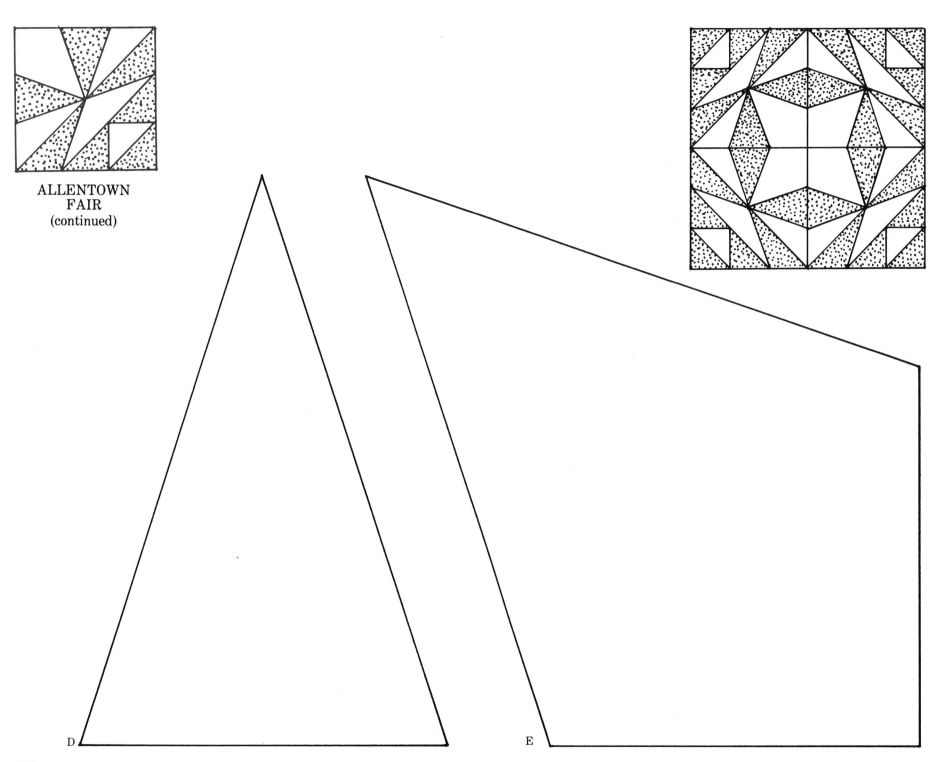

ALLENTOWN
FAIR
(continued)

D

E

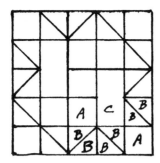

Another traditional pattern re-drawn to use in a four-block wall-hanging; this could be inspiration for the center of a medallion quilt.

Color Recipe: Silvery green, violet-gray, gold, yellow, cream and white, sumac red or rusty orange.

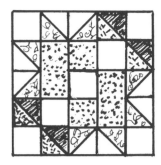

WILDFLOWER MEADOWS©

Add ¼″ seam allowance to all templates.

Cut:
   A 7 background
   A 2 color 4
   B 8 background
   B 8 color 1
   B 4 color 2
   B 4 color 3
   C 2 color 4

Makes 1—10″ block

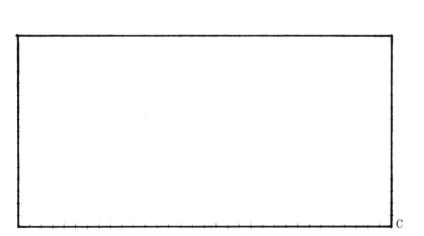

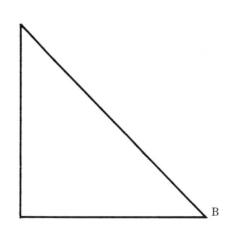

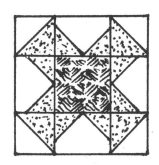

CANADA GOOSE TRACKS

Add ¼″ seam allowance to all templates.

Cut:
- A 1 dark
- B 4 medium
- B 4 light
- C 8 medium
- D 4 light

Makes 1—9½″ block

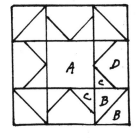

Seen in a quilt shop in North Carolina, this pattern proves that the Canada Goose gets around. Makes a charming scrap quilt.

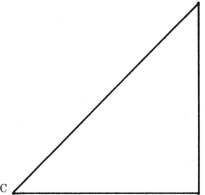

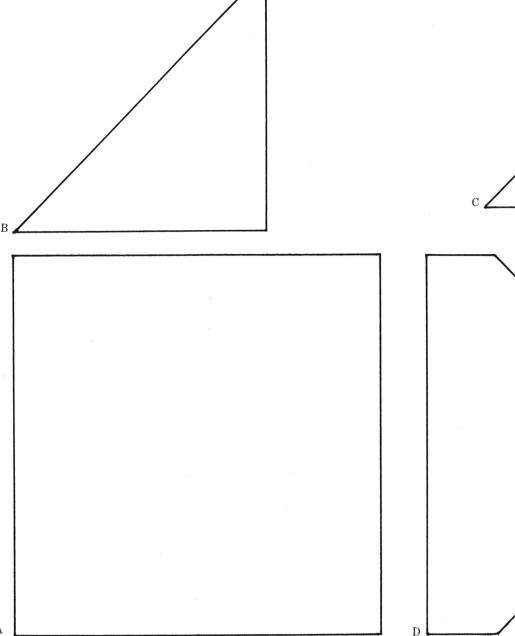

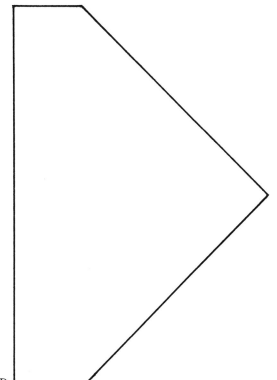

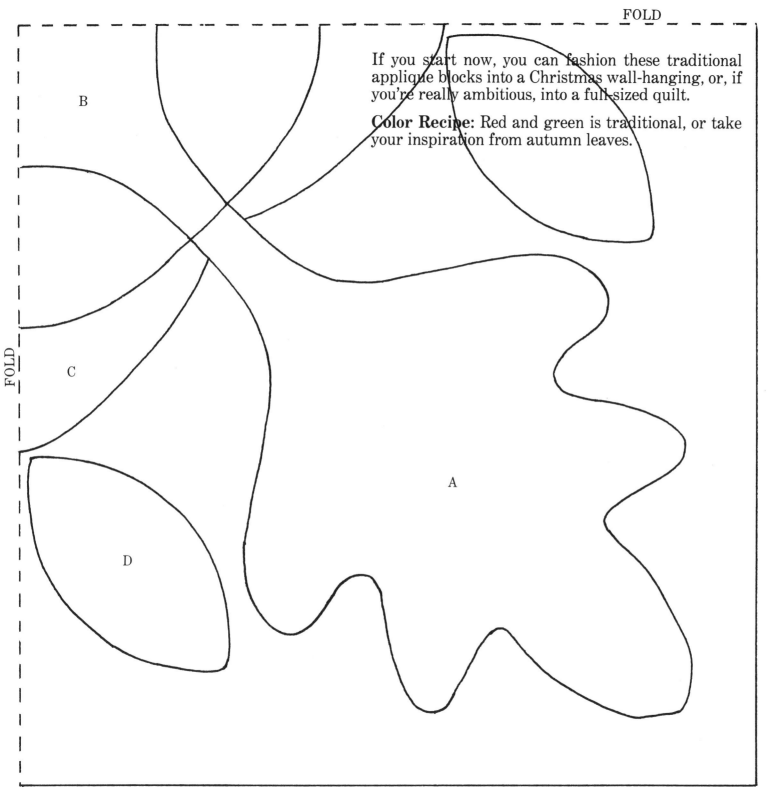

If you start now, you can fashion these traditional applique blocks into a Christmas wall-hanging, or, if you're really ambitious, into a full-sized quilt.

Color Recipe: Red and green is traditional, or take your inspiration from autumn leaves.

OAK LEAF AND REEL

Add ¼″ seam allowance to all templates. Pattern shows one-fourth of a 16″ block.

Cut:
    A 4
    B 1
    C 4
    D 8
    1 background square to finish 16″

Makes 1—16″ block

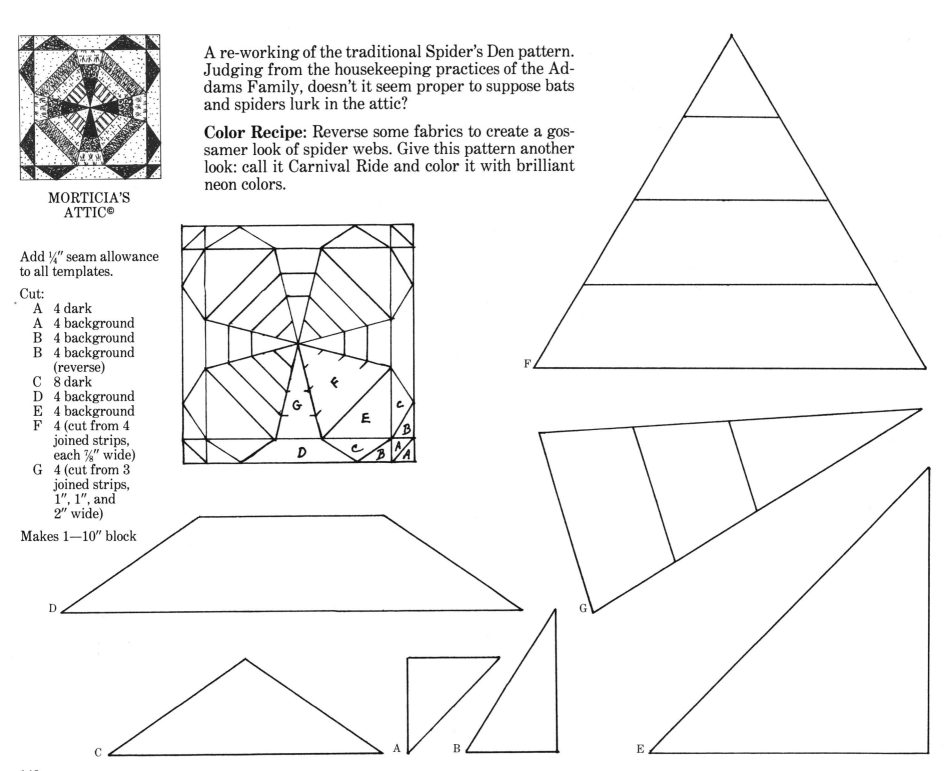

MORTICIA'S ATTIC©

A re-working of the traditional Spider's Den pattern. Judging from the housekeeping practices of the Addams Family, doesn't it seem proper to suppose bats and spiders lurk in the attic?

Color Recipe: Reverse some fabrics to create a gossamer look of spider webs. Give this pattern another look: call it Carnival Ride and color it with brilliant neon colors.

Add ¼″ seam allowance to all templates.

Cut:
- A 4 dark
- A 4 background
- B 4 background
- B 4 background (reverse)
- C 8 dark
- D 4 background
- E 4 background
- F 4 (cut from 4 joined strips, each ⅞″ wide)
- G 4 (cut from 3 joined strips, 1″, 1″, and 2″ wide)

Makes 1—10″ block

As the politicians go 'round and 'round in playing the Election Game, this block too seems to turn.

Color Recipe: Open for debate.

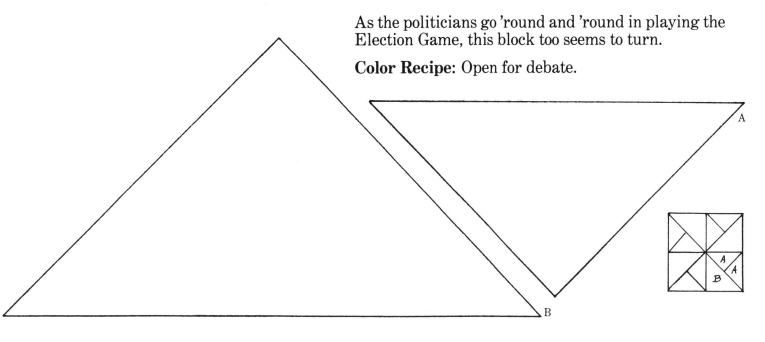

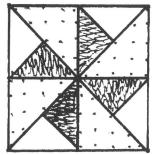

ELECTION
GAME

Add ¼″ seam allowance to all templates.

Cut:
  A 4 color 1
  A 4 color 2
  B 4 color 3

Makes 1—8″ block

By November those winds are blowing rather cold. Make sure you have enough quilts to ward off the winter chill of the Northeast Wind.

Color Recipe: Any color will keep you warm. Do one in hot pink!

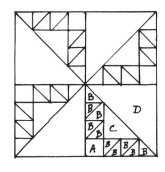

NORTHEAST
WIND

Add ¼″ seam allowance to all templates.

Cut:
  A 4 background
  B 24 medium
  B 16 background
  C 4 dark
  D 4 background

(Continued on page 142)

Makes 1—16″ block

141

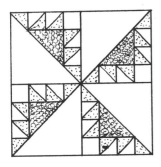

**NORTHEAST
WIND**
(continued)

C

D

With Thanksgiving Day fast approaching, it would behoove the Turkey to use caution and not let his Tracks be seen.

Color Recipe: Let's talk turkey here—you're on your own for color selection.

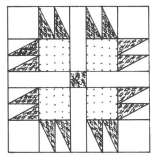

TURKEY TRACKS

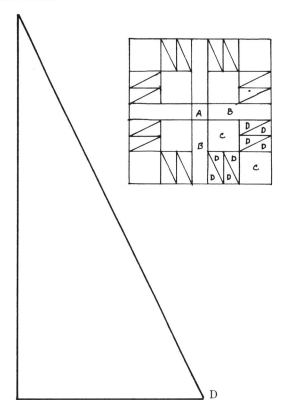

Add ¼″ seam allowance to all templates.

Cut:
- A 1 dark
- B 4 background
- C 4 medium
- C 4 background
- D 16 background
- D 16 dark

Makes 1—18″ block

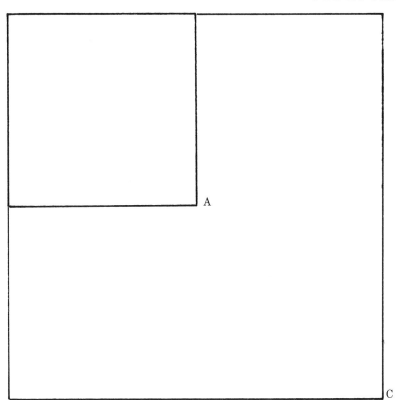

PILGRIM'S JOURNEY©

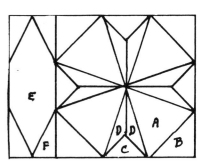

Just as the Pilgrims on their Journey to this land, we too made a new beginning by re-working the traditional Mayflower block.

Color Recipe: Choose colors of a nautical nature, possibly with a subdued quality in keeping with the voyage, or bright colors to express the expectations the end of the journey would bring.

Add ¼″ seam allowance to all templates.

Cut:
    A   4 medium
    B   4 background
    C   4 white
    D   4 light
    D   4 dark (reverse)

For each section of sash cut:
    E   1 white
    F   4 contrast
One 3″ x 3″ square of contrast needed for intersection of 4 blocks.

Makes 1—9″ block and 3″ wide sash.

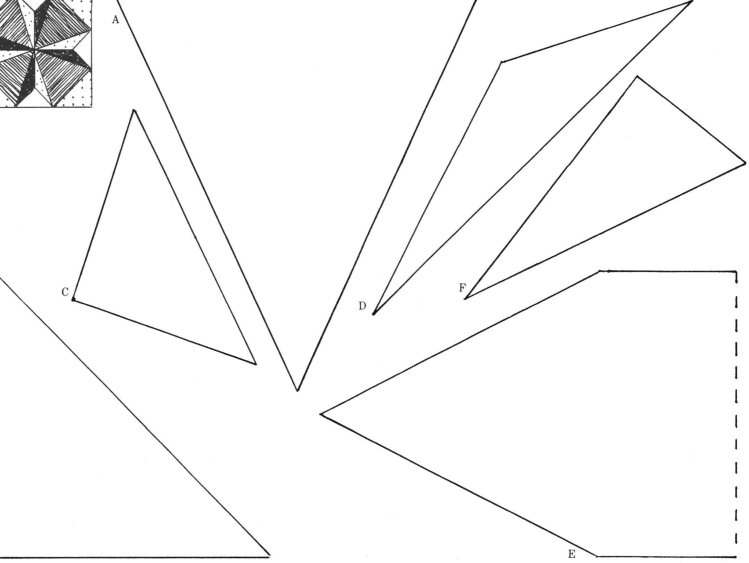

An alternative to applique, this charming teddy has oodles of possibilities. Re-draft to a larger size and use as the center motif for a quilt for a favorite child. Add Bear's Paw or Honey Bee blocks for a border—all bears, even teddies, find honey irresistible.

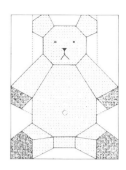

PIECED TEDDY©
BEAR

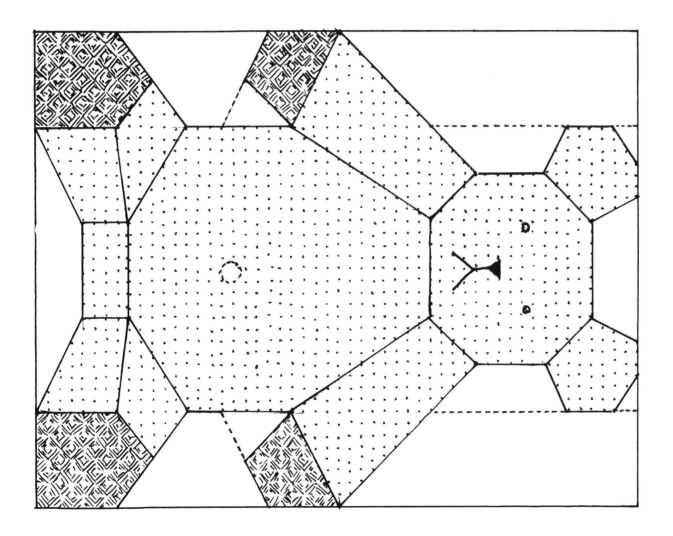

This is a pieced block. Cut templates from actual-size drawing. Add ¼" seam allowance to all templates. Add details with embroidery. Makes 1—5" x 6½" block.

Note: Seams for piecing background are indicated by dotted lines. Some setting in is required when piecing this block. Can be enlarged by drawing a grid over graphic if desired.

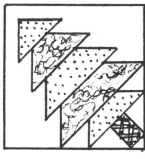

EVERGREEN FIR TREE

When you can't see the forest for the trees or the floor for the fabric, it's time to make a scrap quilt.

Color Recipe: Try this tree pattern using a lot of greens.

Add ¼″ seam allowance to all templates.

Cut:

A 1 background
B 2 background
C 2 background
D 1 brown
E 1 green
F 1 green
G 1 background
G 1 background (reverse)
H 1 green
I 1 background
I 1 background (reverse)
J 1 green
K 1 background
K 1 background (reverse)
L 1 green
M 2 background
N 1 background

Makes 1—10″ block

(Continued on page 147)

146

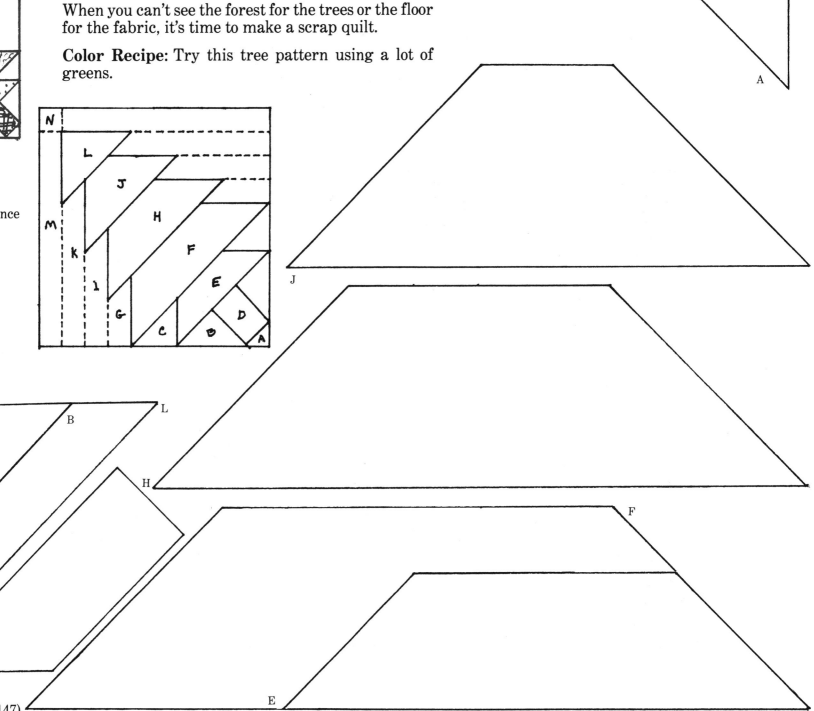

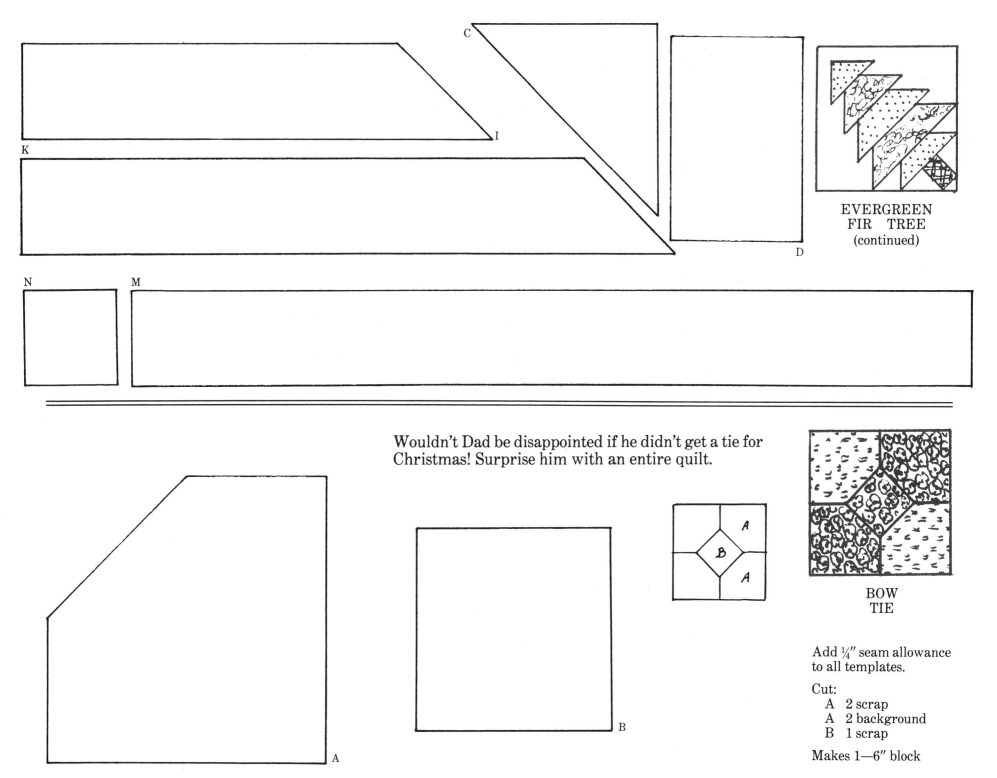

K

I

C

D

N M

EVERGREEN
FIR TREE
(continued)

Wouldn't Dad be disappointed if he didn't get a tie for
Christmas! Surprise him with an entire quilt.

A

B

A
B
A

BOW
TIE

Add ¼″ seam allowance
to all templates.

Cut:
  A   2 scrap
  A   2 background
  B   1 scrap

Makes 1—6″ block

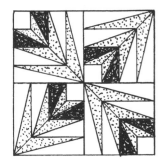

GRANDMOTHER'S
CHRISTMAS
CACTUS

Add ¼″ seam allowance
to all templates.

Cut:
- A   4 background
- B   4 red
- B   4 red (reverse)
- C   4 green
- C   4 green (reverse)
- D   4 background
- D   4 background
    (reverse)
- E   4 green
- E   4 green (reverse)
- F   4 background
- F   4 background
    (reverse)
- G   4 green
- G   4 green (reverse)

Makes 1—16″ block

A little bit of color change moves the Hosannah block
to the Christmas season.

Color Recipe: Green with magenta, pink or red.

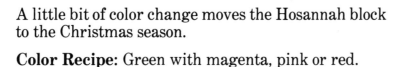

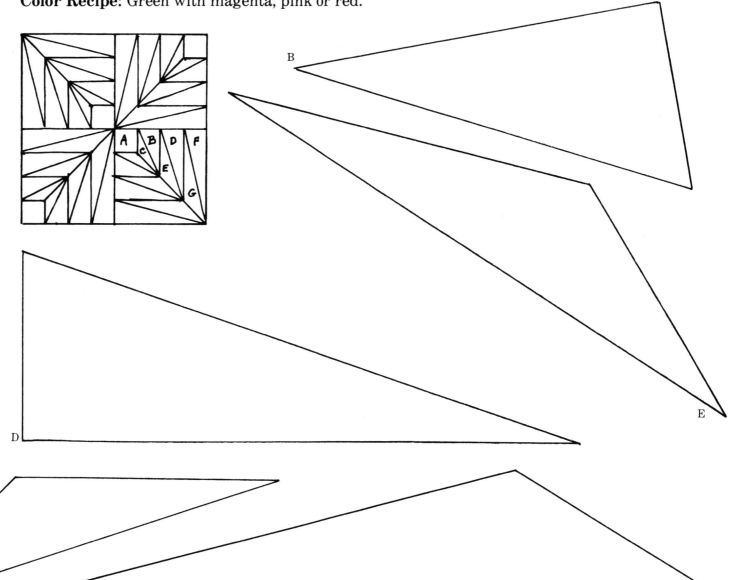

(Continued on page 149)

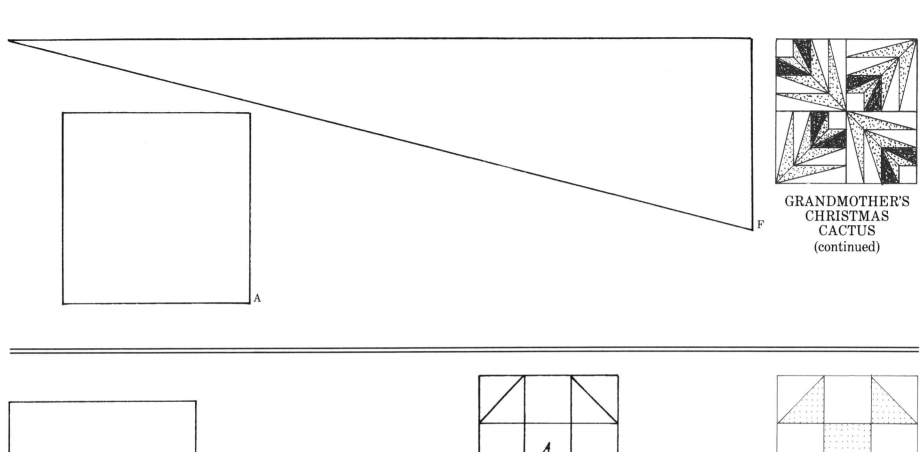

GRANDMOTHER'S
CHRISTMAS
CACTUS
(continued)

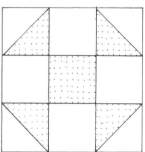

SHOO FLY

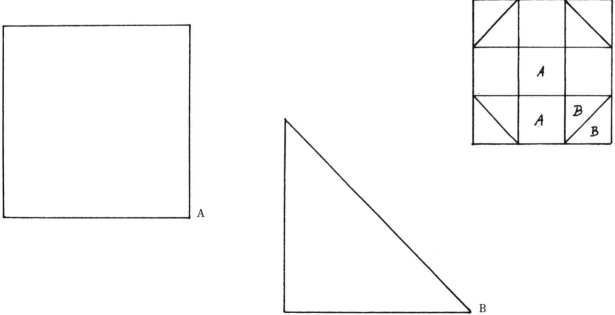

Add ¼″ seam allowance
to all templates.

Cut:
  A 4 light
  A 1 dark
  B 4 light
  B 4 dark

Makes 1—6″ block

STAR OF
STARS©

Add ¼″ seam allowance
to all templates.

Cut:
- A 4 dark
- A 4 dark (reverse)
- B 4 background
- C 5 background
- D 20 background
- E 40 medium
- F 20 background

Makes 1—12″ block

We can hardly think of Christmas or quilt patterns without thinking of stars. The Christmas Star certainly was the Star of Stars. While this block is not especially easy because of its many pieces, persevere and make a Christmas wall-hanging.

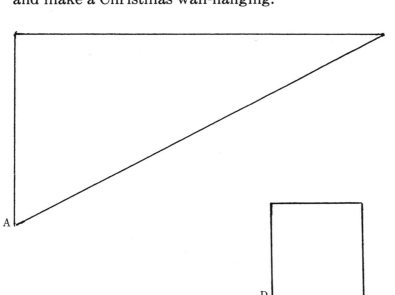

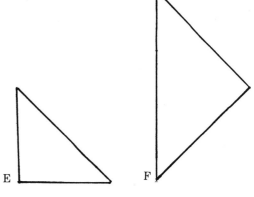

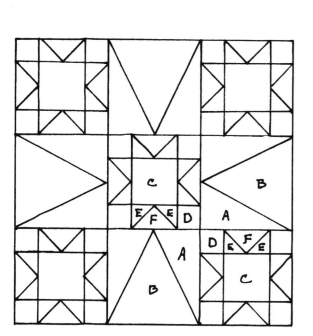

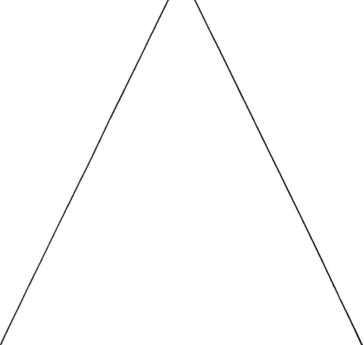

A perfect block to use as a friendship quilt. Have your quilting friends add their names to the hearts in the corner of the block.

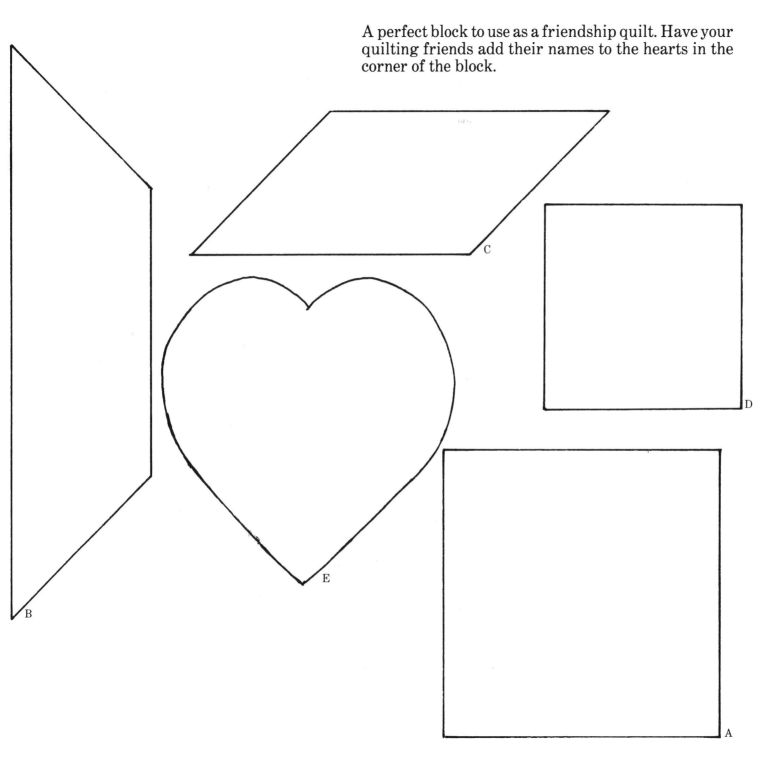

FRIENDSHIP STAR©

Add ¼″ seam allowance to all templates.

Cut:
- A 4 color 1
- B 8 color 2
- C 4 color 3
- C 4 color 4 (reverse)
- D 4 color 1
- E 4 white

Heart template E is appliqued to template A.

Makes 1—12″ block

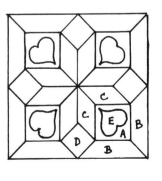

WANDERING VARIABLE STAR©

The Variable Star, as its name implies, appears in numerous forms. So too the Variable Star Quilters are a varied group with a common love of quilting. While their thoughts are often united, they seem to be pursuing various activities and interests which take many to all parts of the country, sometimes even the world. Truly Wandering Variable Stars.

Add ¼″ seam allowance to all templates.

Cut:
- A   4 background
- B   4 background
- B   8 color 1
- C   24 color 2
- C   4 background
- D   4 background
- E   8 color 3
- F   1 background

Makes 1—10″ block

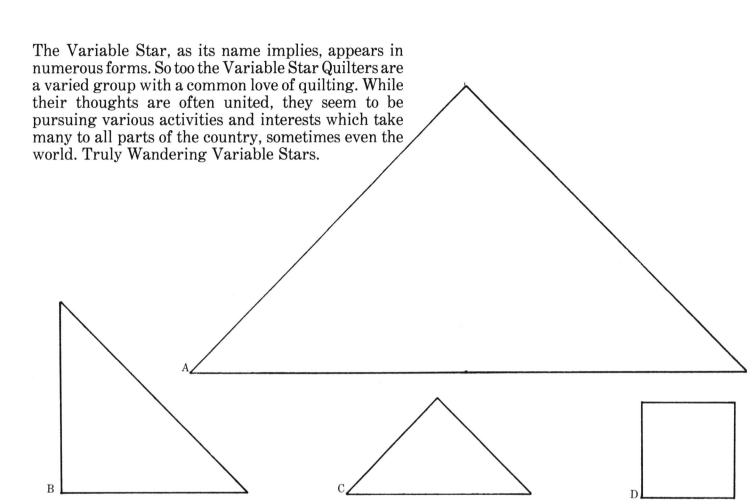

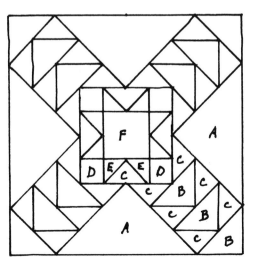

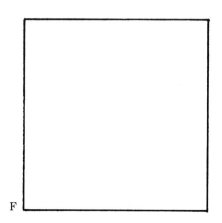

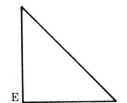

PERKIOMEN HERITAGE©—90″ x 90″

Add ¼″ seam allowance to all templates and measurements given. All numbers given are *finished* size. Refer tc graphic and photo for proper placement of all components.

For center medallion cut and assemble.

    92—3″ split nine-patch blocks cut from templates A and B.

    8—3″ nine-patch blocks of light colors cut from template A.

    Also cut; 1—8½″ x 8½″ block of white (appliqued angel goes on this).

For outer areas cut and assemble:

    24—9″ split nine-patch blocks cut from templates C and D.

    16—9″ half nine-patch blocks cut from templates C and D, of dark colors (4 are for baskets).

    24—9″ half nine-patch blocks cut from templates C and D of light colors.

    Also cut; 2—3″ squares for bases of baskets (cut diagonally to make four).

Template E—8 of white

Template F—4 of white

4—23⅜″ x 25½″ of white (the longer side of this joins to the center medallion but they are not the same length).

4—12¾″ x 12¾″ of white

Folk-art applique motifs are approximately 12¾″ x 12¾″. These are worked on squares of white which are then appliqued in place. Cut out back area to reduce bulk. Basket blocks (half nine-patch) are appliqued onto blocks (template F) after flowers are done. Don't forget the bases.

Dotted lines shown on graphic on page 94 indicate seam lines for piecing white areas.

Nobody said this would be easy.

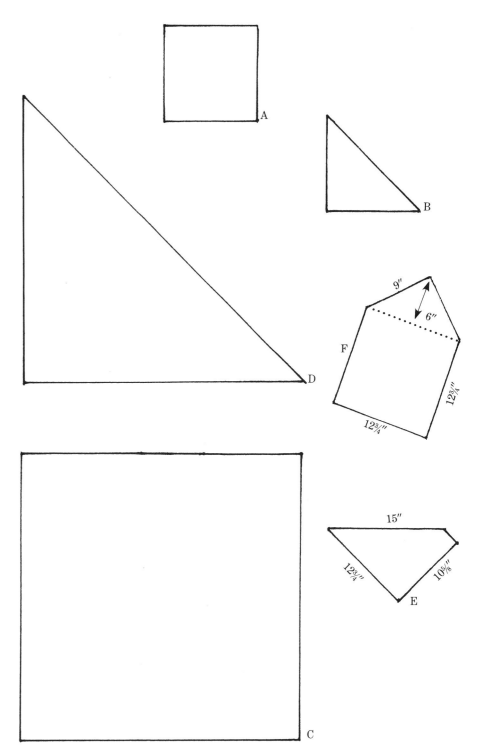

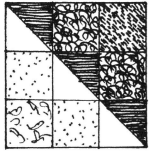

split nine-patch

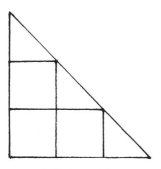

half nine-patch

INDEX—Patterns

INDEX—Recipes

MAIN DISH ENTREE

APPETIZERS

SOUP

INDEX—Recipes (continued)

SALADS

BREADS

DESSERTS